Landmark Visitors Guide

Short Breaks
in Wales

Rita & David Pearson

Published in the UK by:
Horizon Editions Ltd
Trading as The Horizon Press,
The Oaks, Moor Farm Road West, Ashbourne, Derbyshire DE6 1HD
e-mail stella@thehorizonpress.co.uk

1st Edition
ISBN: 978 184306 453 4

Print: Gomer Press Limited. Llandysul, Ceredigion, Wales

Design: Mark Titterton

Front cover: Conwy Castle

Back cover, top: Big Pit, Abergavenny

Back cover, second down: Red Wharf Bay, Beaumaris

Back cover, third down: Caernarfon, Welsh Highland Railway Station

Back cover, bottom: Tenby, Pembrokeshire

Back cover, right: Gower Peninsula, Swansea

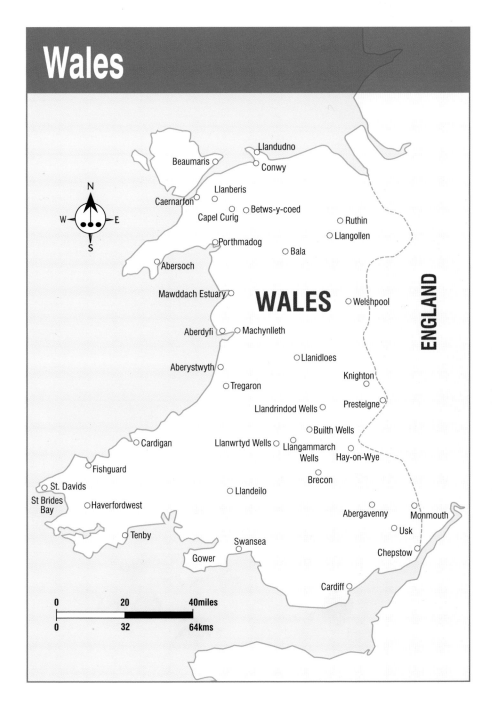

Contents

Opposite page: *Portmeirion*

Welcome to
Short Breaks in Wales

The iconic images of Wales are of rugged mountains, magnificent medieval castles, quaint narrow gauge railways, and spectacular coastline. These features, and more, make Wales an ideal destination for short break holidays.

Waterfall and flowers at Capel Curig Snowdonia

There are two major centres of population, Cardiff and Swansea, featured in this guide, places recently emerged from an industrial past, and now vibrant modern maritime cities well worth a visit.

But Wales is principally a land of open countryside, sprinkled with small towns and villages, rich in historical and cultural heritage; it's an excellent place to relax and unwind, to recharge batteries run down by the hectic pace of modern urban life.

Some of the areas described in the book are well known tourist destinations, such as the ever popular seaside resorts of Tenby and Llandudno and the inland resort of Betws-y-coed. Others are less well known, quiet rural retreats, often with excellent opportunities to explore and enjoy the great outdoors; some with facilities for outdoor adventure activities.

At Dolgellau you can climb majestic Cadair Idris, or hire a bike and ride along the cycle trail beside the beautiful Mawddach estuary. Visit Fishguard in spring to experience the wonderful abundance of wild flowers on the headlands; the walk along the cliff tops to Pwll Deri is a joy. The stunning countryside in Wales is often subtly enhanced by the works of man. The approach to Conwy from the east offers what must arguably be one of the best views in the UK; the estuary with yachts bobbing at their moorings,

the elegant bridges crossing the broad river, the superbly preserved multi-turreted castle, the small town surrounded by high medieval walls, all backed by the lofty mountains of Snowdonia. A little further along the coast the picturesque Menai Strait, separating the island of Anglesey from the mainland, is complemented by the elegance of Telford's suspension bridge. In the Dee Valley the romantic ruins of Dinas Bran castle look down on Llangollen and the Pontcysyllte aqueduct carries narrow boats and fearless pedestrians high above the sparkling river.

The above gives just a glimpse of the treasures of Wales; many more are revealed in the pages of this book.

Landmark Trust

The Landmark Trust is a charity established in 1965 to prevent the loss or irreversible alteration of small but worthwhile buildings of architectural or historical significance. The restored buildings are let as quality holiday accommodation (self catering) to cover on-going maintenance etc. The Landmark Trust has almost 200 properties in its portfolio. Listed are properties within 15 miles of the towns and cities listed in this guide. I suggest you visit the Trust's website where you will be able to find details of the properties and how to make a booking, alternatively:

Booking office:

☎ 01628 825925

email: bookings@landmarktrust.org.uk

www.landmarktrust.org.uk

St Davids Cathedral, Pembrokeshire

Useful Contacts

National Trust (NT):
www.nationaltrust.org.uk

Cadw:
www.cadw.wales.org.uk

National Express:
www.nationalexpress.com

Stagecoach:
www.stagecoachbus.com

Train Enquiries:
www.nationalrail.co.uk
www.thetrainline.com

Transport Direct:
www.transportdirect.info

Top left: *Tenby;* **Top right:** *Aberystwyth pier at sunset;* **Middle:** *Brecon Beacons National Park;*
Bottom left: *Hay-on-Wye;* **Bottom right:** *National Wool Museum, Carmarthenshire;*

Above: *Centre for Alternative Technology (CAT), Machynlleth* **Below:** *Big Pit: National Coal Museum, Blaenafon*

Above: Talyllyn Railway Station, Tywyn

Getting There

By Road

Aberdyfi and Tywyn are on the A493.

By Rail

Both towns are on the Cambrian line from Shrewsbury to Pwllheli

By Coach

There are national coaches to Aberystwyth with a local bus for the onward journey.

Background Briefing

At the southern end of the Snowdonia National Park on the north side of the Dyfi Estuary is the small seaside resort of Aberdyfi; with its smart looking, brightly painted buildings huddled on the hillside this pretty village is a popular destination for visitors. It has miles of sandy beaches with the coveted blue flag and is an ideal spot for water sports and beach games. Watersports include sailing, sail boarding, fishing, boat trips and the summer regatta. There is also an 18 hole championship golf course and Outward Bound Wales is based at Aberdyfi.

To the north is another small seaside town, Tywyn, with a good range of shops and accommodation and four miles of sandy beach. The church of St Cadfans in the centre of the town, parts of which date from the 12th century, is home to an interesting inscribed stone which is the earliest known record of written Welsh, dating from the 8th or 9th century.

Tywyn is also home to the only working Wurlitzer Organ in Wales giving regular public concerts. The Talyllyn narrow gauge railway starts at the Tywyn Wharf Station in town and travels at a gentle 9 miles an hour on a scenic route to Nant Gwernol.

Both resorts make a good base for exploring the delights of the surrounding area especially the Dysynni and Fathew Valleys. The Dysynni Valley is a tranquil and scenic place with a flat valley floor ideal for a pleasant cycle ride. There are two unusual outcrops of rock in the valley, one topped by the ruins of Castell y Bere, built in the 13th century by Llewelyn Fawr (Llewelyn the Great) and Craig yr Aderyn or Bird Rock which has both bronze and Iron Age

fortifications on top. Bird Rock is a great place for bird watchers as it is the breeding ground for a colony of cormorants. Rare birds such as peregrine falcons, choughs and red kites may also be seen. Both have splendid panoramic views of the area.

At the foot of Castell y Bere at Llanfihangel-y-Pennant is the lovely old church of St Michael where there is an exhibition about the local girl Mary Jones, who in 1800 walked from the village the 26 miles/42km to Bala barefoot to obtain a bible in Welsh. Another item of interest is a 14ft long three dimensional cloth map of the Dysynni valley.

At the head of the valley lies Talyllyn Lake nestling beneath Cader Idris; it is thought by many to be one of the most beautiful in Wales. The lake is well known for its excellent trout fishing. At the other end of the valley just north of Tywyn lies the saltwater lagoon Broad Water, a lovely expanse of water noted for bird watching with many wetland birds to be seen.

To the south of Craig yr Adern in the adjacent Fathew Valley are the beautiful Dolgoch waterfalls. They consist of a series of waterfalls which cascade down a rocky wooded ravine into a deep pool below. There is a picnic site at the top and this makes an excellent short walk which can be started from Dolgoch station on the narrow gauge railway.

Attractions Nearby

Talyllyn Railway Company
Wharf Station, Tywyn
LL36 9EY
☎ 01654 710472
www.talyllyn.co.uk
The Talyllyn Railway is one of Wales' best known steam powered narrow gauge railways. It was built

Above Left – Right: Aberdyfi sea front

in 1866 to carry slate from the Bryn Eglwys quarry to the main railway line at Tywyn and the original engines and carriages are still in use today. Talyllyn Railway Preservation Society has owned and run the railway since 1951. It travels for seven and a quarter miles (11.8 km) along the beautiful Fathew valley from Tywyn to Abergynolwyn and Nant Gwernol, passing Dolgoch Falls; the scenery is impressive and there are many walks that can be started from the railway. There are all the facilities you need at the stations of Tywyn and Abergynolwen including parking, shop and refreshments plus at Tywyn there is a narrow gauge railway museum.

Hotels and Dining

Try the local Tourist Information Centre, see Essential Contacts for details.

Something Special

Llety Bodfor

Bodfor Terrace, Aberdovey
LL35 0EA
☎ 01654 767475
www.lletybodfor.co.uk
This 5 star B & B boutique hotel has 8 luxurious bedrooms individually designed by interior designer and owner Ann Hughes. It has stunning views of the Dyfi Estuary and Cardigan Bay.

Trefeddian Hotel

Aberdyfi
LL35 0SB
☎ 01654 767213
www.trefwales.com
The hotel has 15 acres of grounds and overlooks Cardigan Bay. It facilities include a beauty salon, an indoor swimming pool, a tennis court, a games room and a 9 hole putting green.

Penhelig Arms

Aberdyfi
LL35 0LT
☎ 01654 767215
www.penheligarms.com
Set on the waters edge this 18th century inn has a good reputation for food with entries in several good food guides.

Dolgoch Falls Hotel

Bryncrug, Tywyn
LL36 9UW
☎ 01654 782258
The hotel is set in a unique spot at the foot of the Dolgoch Falls and ravine in Snowdonia National Park. It is 5 miles from the coast on the Talyllyn Railway with Dolgoch station 200m behind the hotel.

Cefn Coch Country Guest House,

Llanegryn
Tywyn
LL36 9SD
☎ 01654 712193
www.cefn-coch.co.uk

A 4 star B & B with stunning views of the Dysynni Valley. Also have cycles for hire.

The Bistro on the Square

1 Chapel Square,
Aberdovey
LL35 0EL
☎ 01654 767448
Bistro serving French cuisine.

Events

Summer Regatta Aberdyfi

Essential Contacts

Tywyn Tourist Information Centre
High Street
☎ 01654 710070

Aberdyfi Tourist Information Centre
The Wharf Gardens
LL35 0ED
☎ 01654 767 321

Bird Rock Cycle Hire
Cefn Coch, Llanegryn
Tywyn
LL36 9SD
☎ 01654 712193

Dovey Yacht Club
The Wharf, Aberdyfi
LL35 0EB
☎ 01654 767607

Abergavenny, Monmouthshire

Background Briefing

Situated at the south eastern edge of the Brecon Beacons National Park this charming old market town has traditionally been regarded as a gateway to Wales. It is located in the lush green valley of the River Usk, overlooked by dark brooding mountains.

There is plenty for the outdoor enthusiast and there is much of historical interest from medieval castles to industrial archaeology. Walkers will be attracted by the proximity of the Black Mountains; the town is virtually surrounded by high hills and the three most prominent tops, Skirrid, Sugar Loaf and the Blorenge are popular walking destinations from the town. Blorenge is also regularly used as a launching point for hang and para gliders while the Black Mountains are ideal for pony trekking excursions. A recommended visit is up the beautiful unspoiled Vale of Ewyas, deep in the Black Mountains; wander round the romantic ruins of the Augustinian Priory or don walking boots and climb the steep valley sides to the wild countryside above for an exhilarating ridge walk.

Back in town, connect with the long history of the place by strolling round the ruins of the once powerful castle; visit the museum in the castle grounds and at the nearby Priory Church admire the unique monuments and sculptures, while learning about the priory's long history. There has been a market here since medieval times and this tradition continues, with markets, indoor and out, on several days of the week, the one on Tuesday being the largest. In the evening there are many restaurants available, within the town or in the surrounding countryside, or why not take in a show at the theatre.

Places to visit

Abergavenny Castle and Museum

Castle St, Abergavenny
NP7 5EE
☎ 01873 854282
www.abergavennymuseum.co.uk
The castle, now a picturesque ruin, was an important stronghold for four centuries following its construction by the Norman Lord Hamelin de Ballon in the latter part of the 11th century.

The museum is housed in a former hunting lodge built in the 19th century by the Marquis of Abergavenny within the castle walls. It tells the story of the historic market town from prehistory to the present day and features recreations of a Victorian Welsh farmhouse kitchen and a saddler's workshop.

The Priory Church

Monk St, Abergavenny
NP7 5ND
☎ 01873 853168
www.stmarys-priory.org
Originally part of a Benedictine Abbey, the Priory Church of St Mary is one of the largest and finest parish churches in Wales. Dating chiefly from 14th century the church features superb monuments and sculptures, notably the unique Jesse tree, an impressive larger than life wooden sculpture of the Biblical character, carved in the 15th century. On the same site is the Tithe Barn, restored in 2002, and housing an exhibition exploring a thousand years of the town's history.

Attractions Nearby

Big Pit (8m/12km)

Blaenafon, Caerphilly
NP4 9XP
☎ 01495 790311
www.museumwales.ac.uk
Blaenavon Industrial Landscape was designated a UNESCO world heritage site in 2000. At one of the premier industrial heritage sites in the UK find out about the iron making and coal mining industries that dominated the landscape in the 19th century. The highlight of a visit to Blaenavon has to be a visit to Big Pit Colliery. Don a helmet and cap lamp before entering the cage to descend 300ft/91m into the bowels of the earth for a guided underground tour of the former mine workings; an exciting experience not to be missed.

Above: Abergavenny Castle

Above Left: Big Pit; **Above Right:** Llanthony Priory

Llanthony Priory (13m/21km)

Llanthony

Romantic ruins of an Augustinian Priory in the beautiful unspoiled Vale of Ewyas, deep in the Black Mountains. Plenty of walking opportunities at low or high level.

White Castle

Well preserved medieval fortress in a quiet location 7 miles east of Abergavenny.

Events

Abergavenny Food Festival

www.abergavennyfoodfestival.com

Hotels and Dining

The Angel Hotel

15 Cross Street
NP7 5EN
☎ 01873 857121
An elegant hotel in a former Georgian coaching inn in the centre of town.

For something different try staying in the Castle Lodge. Forming part of the hotel this Victorian lodge at the entrance to the castle can accommodate up to four people with meals taken in the hotel a short walk away; fine views to Blorenge mountain from small private courtyard.

Allt Yr Ynys Country House Hotel & Restaurant (5m/8km)

Walterstone
HR2 0DU
☎ 01873 890307
Centred on a 16th century manor house, once home to Queen Elizabeth I's chief minister, this well appointed hotel offers plenty of activities including an indoor swimming pool, covered clay pigeon shooting and private river fishing in the hotel grounds.

Llanthony Priory Hotel

Llanthony
NP7 7NN
☎ 01873 890487
www.llanthonyprioryhotel.co.uk
This small hotel sits within and is actually part of the 12th century Augustinian Priory. What it may lack in modern amenities it more than makes up for in character. Great base for walking or pony trekking.

Landmark Trust

Clytha Cottage
Lovely folly of 1790 on summit of small hill, sleeps up to 6.

La Brasseria

The Stables , Lewis Lane
NP7 5BA
☎ 01873 737937
Restaurant housed in former stables in town centre.

Abersoch, Gwynedd

Getting There

By Road

M56 and A55 to Bangor, then A487 to Caernarfon and A499 to Abersoch.

By Rail

There are trains from Shrewsbury to Pwllheli then a local bus to Abersoch.

By Coach

There are national coach services to Pwllheli from where a local bus can be caught to Abersoch.

Background Briefing

Abersoch is a small attractive seaside resort on the south coast of the Lleyn Peninsula in north west Wales, with sheltered beaches and beautiful scenery; it is an ideal base for exploring the surrounding area.

It is popular for water sports, such as dingy sailing, wind surfing, and jet skiing, whilst the adjacent beach around the headland at Porth Neigwl (Hell's Mouth) is one of the best surfing beaches in Wales. There are sailing schools, chandlers, surf shops etc. to supply all the needs of water sport enthusiasts plus small shops, restaurants and accommodation for all visitors.

The Lleyn is designated an Area of Outstanding Natural Beauty; it has breathtaking scenery with miles of sandy beaches, interesting coves and windswept headlands. The rolling hills of the Lleyn provide wonderful views of Cardigan Bay, Snowdonia, Anglesey and the Rhinogs and several have the added attraction of iron age hill forts on or near their summits, for example Carn Fadrun a few miles north of Abersoch. A boat trip round the bay to see the seals and other wildlife or to Bardsey Island is something not to be missed in fine weather.

There are many picturesque villages such as Porthdinllaen and Nefyn on the north coast and Aberdaron, the "lands end" of Wales, at the south western tip of the Lleyn.

Pwllheli is a busy market town – market day Wednesday – with a modern marina and leisure centre; to the west of the town is the medieval house of Penarth Fawr.

Places to visit

Boat Trips

Craft and Angling Centre
The Harbour, Abersoch
LL53 7AP
☎ 01758 712646
Boat trips around Abersoch Bay and the bird sanctuaries of St. Tudwals Islands.

Attractions Nearby

Bardsey Island (Ynys Enlli)

www.bardsey.org
Boat Trips can be booked from Pwllheli or Porth Meudwy (4m/6km).
☎ 0 8458 113655
www.enllicharter.co.uk
The island is about 2 miles/3 km off the tip of the Lleyn Peninsular. It is a National Nature Reserve renowned for its wildlife including birds, particularly the Manx shearwater, lichens and flowering plants.

Plas yn Rhiw (NT) (6m/10km)

Rhiw, Pwllheli
LL53 8AB
☎ 01758 780219
A restored manor house and gardens with wonderful views across Cardigan Bay.

Top: Abersoch harbour; Above: Pwllheli seafront

Nefyn and Porthdinllaen (12m/19km)

Attractive villages at opposite ends of a sandy bay on the north coast, there is a maritime museum at Nefyn. Porthdinllaen village and beach are owned by the National Trust and access is on foot only.

Llanbedrog (3m/4.5km)

Another attractive coastal village to the north east. It is home to an award winning arts centre housed in a grade II listed Victorian gothic mansion, with a tearoom and craft shop.

Hotels and Dining

Try the local Tourist Information Centre, see Essential Contacts for details.

Something Special

Tremfan Hall

Llanbedrog
LL53 7NN
☎ 01758 740169
www.tremfanhall.com
A country house with wonderful views; the former home of John Gwenogfryn Evans the founder of the National Library of Wales.

The restaurant uses local produce and advertises excellent service with exciting and varied menus.

Porth Tocyn Country Hotel

Bwlchtocyn, Abersoch
LL53 7BU
☎ 01758 713303
www.porth-tocyn-hotel.co.uk
Award winning country hotel with a restaurant which has the longest lasting continuous entry in the Good Food Guide outside London (51st Year).

Goslings

High Street, Abersoch
LL53 7DY
☎ 01758 712526
www.goslingsabersoch.co.uk
Four star Visit Wales family run hotel in the centre of Abersoch with bistro offering good food, wine and service.

Events

Abersoch Jazz Festival

Abersoch Regatta

SCYC hold many sailing events throughout the summer season.

Wakestock – Europe's largest wakeboard and music festival.

Essential Contacts

Abersoch Tourist information Centre
LL53 7EA
☎ 01758 712929
Email: enquiries@abersochtouristinfo.co.uk

Pwllheli Tourist Information Centre
Min y Don, Sgwar yr Orsaf
LL53 5HG
☎ 01758 613000
Email: pwllheli.tic@gwynedd.gov.uk

SCYC
The Clubhouse, Abersoch
LL53 7DP
☎ 01758 712338
Email: info@scyc.co.uk

Getting There

By Road
The A487 passes north – south through the town. The A44 approaches from the east.

By Rail
The rail station is the terminus of the line from Shrewsbury.

By Coach
A limited coach service is available via Birmingham.

Background Briefing

Situated around the mid-point of the great sweep of Cardigan Bay, Aberystwyth nestles at the foot of low hills where the rivers Rheidol and Ystwyth meet the sea. Despite its modest size it is a town without equal in mid Wales. It has a multi-faceted nature: holiday resort, university town, major administrative centre and regional shopping destination; all co-exist comfortably in this friendly, unpretentious town.

Throughout history Aberystwyth has played a pivotal role in shaping life in Wales: Edward Ist built a powerful castle and walled town in the late 13th century to control the people of the area; the first university in Wales was established in the town in 1872; the National Library of Wales was inaugurated here in 1916 and today the Wales Assembly Government is building a major regional office in the town.

Visitors will be drawn to the broad, paved promenade, 1½ miles long which runs from the harbour, now home to a thriving marina, past elegant, tall Victorian/Edwardian buildings, home to hotels and student accommodation to Constitution Hill. Along the way it passes the once mighty but now ruined castle, the grand neo-Gothic

Top: The seafront; Middle: The church and college buildings from the castle; Bottom: The Castle

original university building, and the foreshortened pier. The beach of shingle and dark sand stretches toward the hill with its electric cliff railway leading to the low summit with marvellous views and fascinating camera obscura. From here the coast footpath may be taken towards Borth; look out for bottlenose dolphins while walking this stretch of Heritage Coast. Other walks may be taken to Pen Dinas Head on the southern edge of town, 374ft/114m high, with an Iron Age fort and great views, or to Parc Penglais, a superb area of woodland above town with beech trees and a fine display of bluebells in spring.

Aberystwyth University is home to over 7000 students and this ensures the town is a bustling, lively place, with plenty of cafes and bars. Small restaurants abound, with cuisine from around the world represented. A visit to the exciting modern Arts Centre is a must, and there is also a cinema and the county museum in town.

As well as the attractions in Aberystwyth itself, it makes a good base for exploring the surrounding countryside. The Vale of Rheidol Railway continues to be a popular tourist draw, carrying visitors the twelve miles to Devil's Bridge, with stunning views along the way and many other destinations in the hinterland and on the coast may be visited by car or local bus.

Places to visit

The National Library of Wales
Aberystwyth
SY 23 3BU
☎ 01970 632800
www.llgc.org.uk
Styled one of the great libraries of the world, this massive and still expanding repository of books, film and art is home to a huge wealth

of knowledge about Wales, and the world.

The library was established in 1907 and since 1916 it has occupied the imposing neo-classical building on Penglais hill overlooking the town. On view to the casual visitor are galleries showcasing treasured manuscripts from the library and a changing programme of art exhibitions. Facilities include a shop selling fine art prints, jewellery and pottery and a restaurant.

Aberystwyth Arts Centre
Aberystwyth University
Penglais Campus
SY23 3DE
☎ 01970 623232
www.aberystwythartscentre.co.uk
Experience theatre productions, cinema, music, dance, art and much more at Wales' largest arts centre. There's something for everyone here at this lively up to the minute venue, part of the University and housed in eye catching modern buildings overlooking the town and Cardigan Bay. Take in a performance at night or during the day browse through the galleries with their touring exhibitions; visit the ceramics gallery, particularly noted for its collection of early 20th century studio pottery, or enjoy a meal in one of the bright modern cafes.

Vale of Rheidol Railway
Park Avenue
SY23 1PG
☎ 01970 625819
www.rheidolrailway.co.uk
Wales is renowned for its 'great little trains' and the Vale of Rheidol Railway is one of the best. It's a narrow gauge, steam hauled route departing from the centre of Aberystwyth and running for 12miles along the beautiful valley to its terminus at Devil's Bridge. Sit back and enjoy the views as the small but powerful engine huffs and puffs up

the steep gradient to its destination. In Devil's Bridge visit the attractive waterfalls and admire the curiously named and formed bridge.

Ceredigion Museum
Coliseum, Terrace Road
SY23 2AQ
☎ 01970 633088
A magnificent restored Edwardian Theatre is home to the county museum. Displays inform about times past in Aberystwyth and the surrounding area.

Attractions Nearby

Bwlch Nant yr Arian Forest Visitor Centre (10m/16km)
Ponterwyd
SY23 3AD
☎ 01970 890694
www.nantyrarian.com
This Forestry Commision venue is probably best known for its programme of red kite feeding; it's a great opportunity to watch these magnificent birds of prey, with feeding taking place every afternoon. Experienced mountain bikers however will be making for one of the trails starting from the visitor centre; all the trails are classed as difficult and vary in length from 5.5m/9km to 22m/35km. For the slightly less energetic there are three way marked walks through the forest ranging in length from 1.2km to 5km. There are also two orienteering courses, an animal puzzle trail, an adventure playground for the children and a café.

Llywernog Silver-lead Mine (11m/17km)
Ponterwyd
SY23 3AB
☎ 01970 890620
www.silverminetours.co.uk
The mining of silver rich lead was once a major industry in this area, particularly in the 19th century. This

museum gives visitors the chance to find out how it was done with a self guided tour around the surface workings and a 45 minute led tour below ground.

Rheidol Hydro Electric Power Station (9m/15km)
Cwm Rheidol
SY23 3NF
☎ 01970 880667
Discover how the forces of nature are harnessed to provide a sustainable source of electricity. The station, run by E.on, is the most powerful of its kind in Wales and England. Guided tours are available and the visitor centre has educational displays and a café.

Plynlimon (13 m/21km to start point)
Not the prettiest but one of the wildest areas of countryside in Wales. Three major rivers, the Severn, the Wye and the Rheidol, have their beginnings in this bleak moorland. If you're into this sort of thing, and a well equipped experienced hill walker, you may be tempted by the challenge of locating and taking a drink from all three sources. Starting point is the Dyffryn Castle Inn near Ponterwyd.

Hafod Estate (20m/31km)
Devil's Bridge
This 800 acre estate in the Ystwyth valley was established in the 18th century. The once grand mansion is long gone but the newly restored paths are a joy to walk with gorges, waterfalls, monuments and varied woodland.

Cors Fochno (Borth Bog) (9m/15km)
Ynyslas , Borth
Not to be missed by nature lovers, or anyone seeking a quiet walk in spectacular scenery, this important nature reserve is the largest area of estuarine raised bog in Britain.

Combine it with a visit to the nearby Ynyslas reserve with its flower rich sand dunes.

Events

Aberystwyth MusicFest

Aberystwyth International Ceramics Festival

Castell Rock

Hotels and Dining

Gwesty Cymru
19 Marine Terrace
SY23 2AZ
☎ 01970 612252
www.gwestycymru.co.uk
Recently renovated hotel with a contemporary Welsh feel, located on the seafront. Local produce is served in the stylishly decorated sea facing restaurant.

Belle Vue Royal
Marine Terrace
SY23 2BA
☎ 01970 617558
www.bellevueroyalhotel.co.uk
Watch the sun go down over Cardigan Bay from this elegant hotel.

Conrah Country House Hotel
Chancery
SY23 4DF
☎ 01970 617941
www.conrah.co.uk

Beautiful rural location, equally convenient for town and country.

Four Seasons Hotel
Portland Street
SY23 2DX
☎ 01970 627458
www.fourseasonshotel.uk.com
Friendly small hotel in town centre.

Little Italy
51 North Parade
SY23 2JN
☎ 01970 625707
www.littleitalyaber.co.uk
Long established and popular Italian restaurant.

The Olive Branch
35 Pier Street
☎ 01970 630572
www.olivebranchrestaurant.co.uk
Intimate Greek taverna.

Essential Contacts

Tourist Information Centre
Lisbourne House, Terrace Road
SY23 2AG
☎ 01970 612125

Commodore Cinema
Bath Street
☎ 01970 612421
www.commodorecinema.co.uk
Family owned, single screen, 410 seat cinema.

Above: Aberystwyth Marina

Getting There

By Road

From the A5 take the A494 to Dolgellau which passes through the centre of Bala.

By Rail

The nearest station is Ruabon on the Shrewsbury to Chester line

By Coach

The X94 Arriva Cymru bus from Chester to Barmouth passes through Bala and also stops at Ruabon railway station.

Background Briefing

Bala is a market town with a wealth of Welsh history and culture, situated in the Snowdonia National Park at the north end of Lake Bala (Llyn Tegid). The town has a variety of shops, restaurants, inns and old buildings. One of the oldest is Neuadd Cyfnod, a restaurant on the main street, formerly the old grammar school. The Norman castle, Tomen y Bala, a mound or motte dating from the 11th to 12th century, is now a garden from the top of which are excellent views of the lake and mountains. The Bala Town Walk (leaflet available from the TIC Bala) covers all the interesting and historic buildings and the leaflet gives a brief history of the town.

Lake Bala is the largest lake in Wales being approximately 4 miles/ 6.4 km long and 1 mile/1.6km wide and the venue for many water sports including sailing, wind surfing, boating and fishing. Not to be missed is the narrow gauge steam railway which runs alongside the lake – Rheilffordd Llyn Tegid (Bala Lake Railway) – a round trip of about 1 hour starting at Llanuwchllyn at the southern end of the lake.

Top: kayaking on Llyn Tegid (Bala Lake); **Middle Left-Right:** Llanuwchllyn Station; Bala Lake Railway; **Bottom:** Canolfan Cywain Centre

There are spectacular views of the lake and surrounding mountains to be seen on this journey.

As well as Lake Bala there is white water rafting, kayaking and canoeing on the Afon Tryweryn in the next valley.

Bala is a good base for touring the mountains of Snowdonia, the Cambrian coast and mid Wales. Pistyll Rhaeadr, the highest waterfall in Wales, situated at the eastern end of the Berwyn Mountains is a beautiful sight well worth seeing.

A visit to Blaenau Ffestiniog for the Llechwedd Slate Caverns makes an interesting day out, with a Victorian village including a pub and sweet shop, a deep mine and a tramway; there is something for everyone.

Places to visit

Rheilffordd Llyn Tegid/ Bala Lake Railway
Llanuwchllyn
LL23 7BD
☎ 01678 540 666
www.bala-lake-railway.co.uk
A scenic 9 mile round trip along the southern edge of Bala Lake, on a narrow gauge steam railway.

Canolfan Cywain Centre
Ysgubor Isaf, Lon y Cariadon
Bala
LL23 7NW
☎ 01678 520920
www.cywain.co.uk
A rural heritage centre with both indoor and outdoor exhibitions, shows and festivals, it also features exhibitions by local artists.

Attractions Nearby

Canolfan Tryweryn (4m/6km)
The National Whitewater Centre
Frongoch, Bala
LL23 7NU
☎ 01678 521083
www.ukrafting.co.uk
The white water centre provides canoeing, kayaking and white water rafting. The river is fed from the nearby Llyn Celyn dam so a fast flowing river is assured. There are adventure breaks and courses provided.

Llechwedd Slate Caverns (18m/29km)
Blaenau Ffestiniog
LL41 4NB
☎ 01766 830306
www.llechwedd-slate-caverns. co.uk
Visit one of Wales's traditional industries at this working slate mine. There is a deep mine tour and a tramway tour plus a Victorian village, Pentre Llechwedd, complete with pub and sweet shop. The deep mine and tramway tours are open all year round and the village, which has free admission, is open from March to September.

Pistyll Rhaeadr (15m/24km)
www.pistyllrhaeadr.co.uk
Take the B4391 from Bala to Llanrhaeadr ym Mochnant and follow the signs.
Pistyll Rhaeadr is one of the seven wonders of Wales, at 240ft/74m it is the highest waterfall in England and Wales. Its remote location at the western end of the Berwyn Mountains near the village of Llanrhaeadr ym Mochnant is well worth the visit.

Hotels and Dining

Try the local Tourist Information Centre, see Essential Contacts for details.

Fron Dderw Country House Hotel
Stryd y Fron, Bala
LL23 7YD
☎ 01678 520301
www.fronderrwhouse.co.uk
17th century mansion with views of Bala Lake and the Berwyn Mountains. Local produce and fine wines are a speciality of the restaurant. It is an adult friendly hotel so no children under 12.

White Lion Royal Hotel
High Street, Bala
LL23 7AE
☎ 01678 520314
Visit Wales 4 star inn with a popular restaurant.

Plas Coch
High Street. Bala
LL23 7AB
☎ 01678 520309
www.plascoch.com
An historic coaching inn dating from about 1780.

Something Special

Pale Hall
Pale Estate, Llanderfel
LL23 7PS
☎ 01678 530285
www.palehall.co.uk
Luxurious Victorian country house hotel set in 16 acres of gardens. Holder of The True Taste of Wales silver food and drink award. British and French modern and classic cuisine.

Neuadd Cyfnod
High Street, Bala
LL237PG
☎ 01678 521269
Restaurant situated in the old grammar school one of the oldest buildings in Bala, renowned for the quality of its food.

Events

Wa Bala – music festival featuring Welsh Bands

Essential Contacts

Bala Tourist Information Office
Penllyn, Bala
LL23 7SR
☎ 01678 521021

Bala Cinema / Sinema Neuadd Buddug
Town Hall, Bala
LL23 7SR
☎ 01678 520800

Bala Leisure Centre
Pensarn Road, Bala
LL23 7SR
☎ 01678 521222

Bala Adventure & Watersports Centre
Bala Lake
LL23 7SR
☎ 01678 521 059
www.balawatersports.com

Beaumaris, Anglesey

Getting There

By Road
A55 to Britannia Bridge, then A545 to Beaumaris.

By Rail
Beaumaris can be reached by local bus from Bangor Station, on the Chester to Holyhead line.

By Coach
Coach to Bangor then onward by local bus.

Background Briefing

This historic seaside town lies at the northern edge of the Menai Strait where the turbulent waters that separate the Isle of Anglesey from the mainland meet the open sea. A popular tourist destination since Victorian times it offers unrivalled views across the water to the mountains of Snowdonia.

The fairytale, moated, Beaumaris Castle is well preserved and a joy to behold; at the time of its building in the late 13th century it was state-of-the-art in terms of its concentric design, but curiously it was never quite finished. While the castle is the best known attraction in town the more recent historical buildings of the old courthouse and the stark Victorian Gaol are well worth a visit.

From the town pier boat trips can be taken either around Puffin Island, to view the seabirds and seals, or into the Menai Strait where you will have a chance to admire close at hand the two stately bridges crossing the Strait. Telford's elegant suspension bridge, opened in 1826 provided the first direct link to the island and still carries traffic today; Robert Stevenson's sturdy tubular railway bridge followed in 1850 but following a disastrous fire in 1970 it was rebuilt as a remarkable double decker, arched construction, carrying the busy A55 trunk road above the rail track.

Beaumaris is a good place to use as a base for exploring the Isle of Anglesey. The island has a well deserved reputation for having some of the best beaches in North Wales: families love the long sandy beach at Benllech; Red Wharf and Llanddona are ideal for beach games; at Llanddwyn walk out to the island with its quiet coves and old lighthouse, the perfect place for a picnic on a fine summer's day.

The forest at Newborough, on the way to Llanddwyn, is a good place to look out for red squirrels. This delightful creature, no longer present in most of Britain, is thriving on Anglesey; they are most numerous in Newborough Forest and the woods behind Red Wharf Bay but they have even been spotted in the environs of Beaumaris.

A little further away South Stack, near Holyhead, is a popular destination with its spectacular rock formations, abundant bird life and the chance to visit the lighthouse on its craggy islet. The RSPB have a visitor centre here at the top of the cliffs with binoculars and telescopes provided for viewing the nesting sea birds.

Above: Moelfre

Places to visit

Beaumaris Gaol
Steeple Lane
LL58 8EP
☎ 01248 810921
Follow in the footsteps of thieves and murderers at this grim Victorian goal; see the treadmill, the condemned cell and the gibbet.

Beaumaris Court
Castle Street
LL58 8BP
☎ 01248 811691
Staying with the theme of crime and punishment, visitors can explore the historic Courthouse, built in 1614 and last used in 1971. Learn about some of Anglesey's notorious criminals and experience standing in the dock.

Beaumaris Castle
Castle St, Beaumaris
LL58 8AP
☎ 01248 810361
Without doubt Beaumaris' most visited attraction, the castle is a building of great beauty, enhanced by its rural setting on the edge of town and its moat with swans and ducks. Explore the narrow passageways, visit the tranquil vaulted chapel and enjoy a walk on the walls with amazing views of the island, the sea and the Snowdonia mountains.

Attractions Nearby

Penmon Priory (4m/6km)
Penmon
A peaceful place steeped in history with a 12th century church containing impressive Celtic crosses, an ancient holy well, and an intriguing vaulted stone dovecote. Soak up the atmosphere in this rural location, barely touched by the modern world.

Plas Newydd (NT) (7m/12km)
Llanfairpwll
LL61 6DQ
☎ 01248 715272
Superbly situated in extensive gardens on the shore of the Menai Strait, this grand mansion, home of the Marquis of Anglesey, features an important display of work by the painter Rex Whistler, who stayed at the house in the 1930s.

Anglesey Sea Zoo (11m/18km)
Brynsiencyn
LL61 6TQ
☎ 01248 430411
Wales' largest aquarium has something for all the family with the emphasis on species found around local shores, from lobsters to sharks, and strongly influenced by conservation issues.

Oriel Ynys Mon (14m/22km)
Rhosmeirch, Llangefni
LL77 7TQ
☎ 01248 724444
The centre contains two galleries devoted to local history and to art. The art gallery features work by wildlife artist Charles Tunnicliffe and also the largest collection of paintings by renowned local landscape artist Sir Kyffin Williams.

Beaumaris Castle

Left: Plas Newydd
Above: Irish band at the Old Court House
Right: Menai Bridge
Below: Llanfair PG, the UK's longest placename

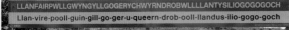

LLANFAIRPWLLGWYNGYLLGOGERYCHWYRNDROBWLLLLANTYSILIOGOGOGOCH
Llan-vire-pooll-guin-gill-go-ger-u-queern-drob-ooll-llandus-ilio-gogo-goch

Menai Bridge (4m/7km)

This small settlement, situated at the narrowest point of the Menai Strait, was known as Porthaethwy before the building of the bridge. Wander along the waterfront to see the small islands linked to the mainland by causeways, but above all admire the two wonderful bridges leaping across the fast flowing and treacherous waters.

South Stack (29m/45km)

Observe the birds from the RSPB visitor centre at Ellin's Tower, wander along the cliff paths, or climb down the 400 steps cut into the cliff face to visit the lighthouse.

Hotels and Dining

Try the local Tourist Information Centre, see Essential Contacts for details.

Something Special

Cleifiog B+B

Townsend, Beaumaris
LL58 8BH
☎ 01248 811507
www.cleifiogbandb.co.uk
Sumptuously decorated and furnished 5 star B and B, with 18th century pine panelling, in a historic house on the sea front, originally a hospice run by monks.

Bishopsgate House Hotel

54 Castle Street
LL58 8BB
☎ 01248 810302
www.bishopsgatehotel.co.uk
Fully restored 18th century Georgian town house in the centre of town.

Tre-Ysgawen Hall Country House Hotel and Spa (13m/21km)

Capel Coch, Llangefni
LL77 7UR
☎ 01248 750750
www.treysgawen-hall.co.uk
With four poster beds, indoor swimming pool, sauna, steam room and gym, this hotel is housed in a grand 19th century country mansion sat within landscaped gardens.

Ye Old Bulls Head

Castle Street
LL58 8AP
☎ 01248 810329
www.bullsheadinn.co.uk
This historic coaching house in the centre of town offers locally sourced British dishes with fine dining in the loft restaurant or a more informal, child friendly atmosphere in the brasserie.

Courts Restaurant

Regent House, Church Street
LL58 8AB
☎ 01248 810565
www.courtyardcuisine.com
Welsh and international cuisine in modern surroundings in a central location.

Events

Beaumaris Arts Festival

www.beaumarisfestival.co.uk

Anglesey Walking Festival

www.angleseywalkingfestival.com

Getting There

By Road
Situated on the A5 between Llangollen and Bangor.

By Rail
The Conwy Valley line from Llandudno to Blaenau Ffestiniog passes through Betws-y-coed.

By Coach
There are national coach/bus services to Conwy, then local bus or train.

Background Briefing

Betws-y-coed is a popular and bustling village in the Conwy Valley at the heart of the Snowdonia National Park. Developed by the Victorians it is much visited for its beautiful setting surrounded by Gwydir Forest Park; it has picturesque rivers dashing down rocky gorges and world famous waterfalls. The Rivers Llugy, Lledr, Machno and Conwy provide pretty and spectacular walks of varying lengths, one of the best being from Pont y Pair in the centre of the village to the renowned Swallow Falls and another is the walk to Conwy Falls and Fairy Glen to the south of the village.

Along with nearby Capel Curig the village caters for all outdoor enthusiasts, with mountain bike trails, walks of all types from gentle river strolls to the mountains of Snowdonia and other outdoor activities too. Capel Curig is the home of the National Mountain Centre, Plas y Brenin, where there are holidays and courses for every conceivable outdoor activity available. The village has many shops selling clothing, outdoor gear and crafts as well as cafés, restaurants and

Top: Shopping area at the Railway Station; **Middle:** Pont y Pair; **Bottom:** The Ugly House

accommodation to suit all tastes.

On the banks of the River Conwy is the 14th century St Michaels Church. The oldest building in the village, it was rescued and is now maintained by the Friends of St Michaels; it is a quiet and peaceful place to visit. At the railway station as well as the Conwy Valley line to Llandudno and Blaenau Ffestiniog there is a miniature railway and museum. Across the car park from the station is the Snowdonia National Park Centre with lots of tourist information and adjacent is a small Motor Museum displaying a variety of old vehicles from the Houghton family collection, some quite rare.

On the A5 between Betws-y-coed and Capel Curig is the much visited Ugly House, home of the Snowdonia Society.

Along the A470 just to the south of the village is Dolwyddelan Castle, one of the surviving castles of the native Welsh princes

An interesting short trip up the Conwy Valley could include Llanrwst, a small market town with a 16th century bridge thought to be designed by Inigo Jones, at the end of which is the often photographed Ty Hwnt i'r Bont, a 15th century cottage now a NT tearoom. Trefriw Woollen Mill, Gwydir Castle, a Tudor courtyard house, Gwydir Uchaf chapel with its painted ceiling and Capel Garmon Neolithic Chambers are all nearby.

Places to visit

Conwy Valley Railway Museum

The Old Goods Yard
Betws-y-coed
LL24 0AL
☎ 01690 710568
www.conwyrailwaymuseum.co.uk
7¼ inch gauge miniature railway with steam engines and an electric tramcar. There is also a museum, model shop and café.

Betws-y-coed Motor Museum

Betws-y-coed
LL24 0AH
☎ 01690 710760
www.ukattraction.com/north-wales/betws-y-coed-motor-museum.htm
A varied collection of motor vehicles including motor bikes and motoring memorabilia.

The Marin Mountain Bike Trail

Gwydyr Forest, Betws-y-coed
Bike hire from Beics Betws
☎ 01690 710 766
www.bikewales.co.uk/
A challenging 25 km mountain bike trail to the North of the village.

Saint Michaels Church

Old Church Road, Betws-y-coed
☎ 01690 710333
www.stmichaelsbyc.org.uk

Attractions Nearby

The Ugly House (3m/5km)

Capel Curig
LL24 0DS
☎ 01690 720287
www.snowdonia-society.org.uk
An ancient cottage with an interesting history, it has an organically managed wildlife garden and several acres of woodland walks.

Above: Fairy Glen, Betws-y-coed; **Top right:** Tŷ Mawr (NT) above Penmachno; **bottom:** Gwydir Castle, Llanrwst

The National Mountain Centre (6m/10km)

Plas y Brenin, Capel Curig

LL24 0ET

☎ 01690 720214

www.pyb.co.uk

The place to visit for everything outdoors: hill walking, climbing, mountain biking, kayaking, taster sessions, family activity courses. You can hire equipment at the centre.

Ty Mawr Wybrnant (NT) (5m/8km)

Penmachno, Betws-y-coed

LL25 0HJ

☎ 01690 760213

www.attractions-north-wales.co.uk/attraction.asp?loc=16

A 16th century traditional stone built farmhouse, birthplace of Bishop William Morgan who was the first person to translate the bible into Welsh.

Trefriw Woollen Mills (7m/11km)

Main Road, Trefriw

LL27 0NQ

☎ 01492 640462

www.t-w-m.co.uk

A working woollen mill producing traditional Welsh bedspreads and tweeds. You can tour the mill and there is a mill shop and café.

Hotels and Dining

Try the local Tourist Information Centre, see Essential Contacts for details.

Something Special

Tan y Foel Country House

Capel Garmon, Betws-y-coed

LL26 0RE

☎ 01690 710507

www.tyfhotel.co.uk

This small family run WTB 5 star gold award winning guest house offers unique, quiet, luxury accommodation, with sweeping views of the Conwy Valley. Its restaurant

Llyn Geirionydd above Trefriw

has 3 rosettes in the AA Restaurant Guide plus many other awards.

Landmark Trust

Rhiwddolion

Three small cottages, isolated at head of valley, sleep 2,3,4.

Craig-y-Dderwen

The Riverside Hotel

Betws-y-coed

LL24 0AS

☎ 01690 710293

www.snowdoniahotel.com

16 acres of gardens on the bank of the River Conwy. The kitchen garden produces vegetables, salads, herbs, fungi, fruit and edible flowers for the restaurant, which has an AA rosette for culinary excellence.

Ty Gwyn Hotel

Betws-y-coed

LL24 0SG

☎ 01690 710383

www.tygwynhotel.co.uk

This multi award winning former coaching inn which has been recently re-furbished is renowned for its international cuisine and uses fresh local produce.

Bistro Betws-y-coed

Holyhead Road

LL240AY

☎ 01690 710328

www.bistrobetwsycoed.demoweb4-u.co.uk

Family run bistro with award winning chefs, specialising in traditional Welsh and modern dishes

Brecon, Powys

Getting There

By Road
On the junction of the A40 and A470.

By Rail
The nearest train stations are Abergavenny or Merthyr Tydfil.

By Coach
National coach and bus services go to Brecon.

Background Briefing

This charming small town, nestling at the foot of the Brecon Beacons, has something to offer all visitors. An historic market town with fascinating narrow streets and alleyways, Georgian shop fronts and wonderful views of the Beacons, there are two museums, the Brecknock Museum and the South Wales Borderers Museum and a cathedral with Norman origins. You can enjoy a trip on the Monmouthshire and Brecon Canal or a visit to the modern theatre both located at the canal basin. The town has all the facilities for visitors, plenty of places to eat and stay, plus an excellent leisure centre with swimming pool.

The Taff Trail, a mostly traffic free route for walkers and cyclists, runs from Cardiff Bay through the Valleys to finish at Brecon.

For the outdoor enthusiast the Brecon Beacons National Park beckons, there are mountains with Pen y Fan, the highest in south Wales, being the nearest. Waterfall country at the Southern edge of the National Park near Ystradfellte has some spectacular waterfalls in scenic valleys plus nearby is the cave Porth yr Ogof. A short journey to the east is Llangorse Lake where all manner of water sports and activities can be found.

Above: Brecon Beacons National Park; **Below:** Talybont Reservoir, near Brecon

Fourteen miles down the A40 is Crickhowell a small market town in the Usk Valley, set between the Black Mountains and the Beacons and with a 16th century bridge across the river, it provides many photo opportunities. It is well known for its variety of places to eat and is something of a gourmet centre in the area.

Places to visit

Brecon Cathedral

The Cathedral Office
The Cathedral Close, Brecon
LD3 9DP
www.breconcathedral.org.uk
The cathedral has a long history, a priory being founded on the site in 1093; this later became the Parish church in the 16th century and finally a cathedral in 1923. There is a heritage centre which illustrates the history and life of the cathedral; the heritage centre itself being housed in an old restored tithe barn makes an interesting visit.

Brecknock Museum & Art Gallery

Captain's Walk, Brecon
LD3 7DS
☎ 01874 624121
The museum which is housed in the Old Shire Hall gives an insight of the history, natural history and art of the area. The gallery has a collection of Welsh art including the work of modern artists.

South Wales Borderers Museum

The Barracks, Brecon
LD3 7EB
☎ 01874 613310

www.rrw.org.uk
The House has a fine collection reflecting the regiment's 300 year history, the highlight of which is the Zulu War room. There is a shop selling a wide range of books and souvenirs about the regiment and the Zulu War.

Theatre Brycheiniog

Canal Wharf, Brecon
LD3 7EW
☎ 01874 611622
www.theatrbrycheiniog.co.uk
Brecon theatre has an extensive programme of events including plays, concerts and festivals to suit all tastes.

Dragonfly Cruises

☎ 07831 685222
www.dragonfly-cruises.co.uk
A cruise on this scenic canal is a delight; the canal follows the valley above the River Usk.

Attractions Nearby

Llangorse Lake (6m/10km)

www.brecon-beacons.com/llangorse-lake.htm
The largest lake in south Wales, it is a SSSI and a haven for wildlife. There are many activities at the lake including coarse fishing and all manner of watersports. Boats from pedaloes to boats for fishing can be hired.

Brecon Mountain Railway (19m/31km)

☎ 01685 722988
www.breconmountainrailway.co.uk
Located just off the Heads of the Valleys trunk road – about 3 miles north of Merthyr Tydfil. Follow the Mountain Railway signs from the A470 and A465 and you arrive in the large free car park.
Seated in one of the observation coaches, a vintage steam locomotive will haul you through the

Top left: The taff trail footpath and cycle route alongside the Monmouthshire and Brecon Canal; Top right: Llangorse lake; Above: Brecon Theatre

Penpont, Brecon

beautiful scenery of the Brecon Beacons National Park along the edge of Taf Fechan Reservoir to Dol-y-Gaer.

Hotels and Dining

Try the local Tourist Information Centre, see Essential Contacts for details.

The Coach House

12 – 13 Orchard Street, Brecon
LD3 8AN
☎ 01874 620043
www. coachhousebrecon.com
A WTB and AA 5 star highly commended contemporary town house B & B totally refurbished in 2007.

The George Hotel

George Street, Brecon
LD3 7LD
☎ 01874 623421
www. george-hotel.com

Something Special

Peterstone Court Hotel

Llanhamlach, Brecon
LD3 7YB
☎ 01874 665387
www. peterstone-court.com

This country house and spa has an impressive Georgian exterior, large airy rooms with a modern touch and a beautiful backdrop of the Beacons. The meat and poultry for the restaurant is reared on the family farm 7 miles away and seasonal local fresh produce is used.

Castle of Brecon Hotel

The Castle Square, Brecon
LD3 9DB
☎ 01874 624611
www.breconcastle.co.uk
Newly restored Georgian restaurant serving modern and traditional cuisine prepared with locally sourced produce.

Ty Croeso Hotel & Restaurant

The Dardy, Crickhowell
NP8 1PU
☎ 01873 810573
Ty Croeso Restaurant is listed by Les Routiers and has been awarded an AA rosette AA★★ WTB★★★ & Green Dragon Award.

Events

Brecon Jazz Festival

www.breconjazz.co.uk

World famous international jazz festival which has been filling the town of Brecon for 25 years at the beginning of August.

Essential Contacts

Brecon Tourist Information Centre
The Market Car Park
Brecon
LD3 9DA
☎ 01874 622485

Brecon Leisure Centre
Penlan, Brecon
LD3 9SR
☎ 01874 623677
www.brecon-leisurecentre.powys.gov.uk

National Park Visitor Centre
Libanus, Brecon
LD3 8ER
☎ 01874 623366
www.breconbeacons.org

Getting There

By Road
Take the A55 or the A5 to Bangor and then the A487 to Caernarfon.

By Rail
The nearest station is Bangor then onwards by frequent local bus service.

By Coach
Limited national coach service to Caernarfon.

Left: The Castle; Right: One of the narrow streets within the town walls

Background Briefing

Caernarfon, positioned between the Menai Strait and Snowdonia National Park, is a busy market town. There are narrow streets, ancient gateways and the town walls, which give the town character, plus shops, restaurants, old pubs and a scenic harbour. The Welsh Highland Railway starts near the castle and the harbour and Victoria Dock overlooking the Menai Strait has plenty for visitors to see.

Although the town is dominated by its magnificent castle, still largely intact after 700 years, and with its polygonal towers, towering battlements and colour banded masonry it is a striking sight, there are many more reasons to visit. The town is much older than its mediaeval castle, certainly the Romans were here in the first century AD and today you can visit the fort they built, Segontium and a small museum nearby which tells the story of the Roman conquest and displays artefacts from the fort.

Caernarfon is also well placed for visiting the Lleyn Peninsula with its pretty coastal villages and scenic coastline, Snowdonia National Park and the coastal resorts of North Wales, plus there are many attractions both in the town and nearby.

Places to visit

Caernarfon Castle (Cadw)
Caernarfon Castle, the most impressive and commanding of Edward Ist's castles, along with the town walls is a World Heritage Site. The castle also houses the Regimental Museum of the Royal Welch Fusiliers.

Doc Fictoria
www.docfictoria.co.uk
Doc Fictoria is just a stone's throw from the town walls alongside a Blue Flag marina. It was built in the 1870s to transport Welsh slate but with the decline of the slate industry it gradually fell into disuse until its recent redevelopment into a yachting marina. There are bustling bars and bistros, fashionable cafés and restaurants, a maritime museum and an attractive range of shops and stores including the Celtica Retail Centre, which specialises in all things Celtic. It is also the home of the award winning Y Galeri Arts Centre which has a theatre, cinema and art space and features a varied programme of events.
www.galericaernarfon.com

Welsh Highland Railway
Ffestiniog & Welsh Highland Railways, Harbour Station, Porthmadog

LL49 9NF
☎ 01286 677018 (Caernarfon booking office)
☎ 01766 516000
www.welshhighlandrailway.net
This narrow gauge railway is due to link up to the Ffestiniog Railway in late 2009; passengers will then be able to make a trip of 40 miles from Caernarfon to Blaenau Ffestiniog via Porthmadog. The trains, some hauled by steam locomotives, run from the centre of Caernarfon through some of the most spectacular scenery in Snowdonia.

Attractions Nearby

Caernarfon Airworld Museum (7.5 m/12.5 km)
Dinas Dinlle, Caernarfon
LL54 5TP
☎ 01286 830800
www.air-world.co.uk/Museum
Caernarfon airfield was of great importance during World War II, used for training the air crews of Bomber Command. The hands on museum has a large collection of aircraft including the Hunter, Seahawk, Javelin and Vampire plus the Westland Whirlwind helicopter, and visitors are able to sit in some of the cockpits. Pleasure flights are also run from the airport.

Parc Glynllifon (6m/10km)

Ffordd Clynnog, Llandwrog
LL54 5DY
☎ 01286 830222
Glynllifon is one of three Grade I listed gardens in Gwynedd.

The seventy acre gardens are home to many specimens of unusual trees. Small follies, including the Mill, Hermitage and the Boathouse are dotted around the grounds along with several modern sculptures. The restored static steam engine is one of the oldest working engines in Britain. There is also a gallery, workshops, craft shop & cafe in the park.

Inigo Jones Slate Works (5m/8km)

Groeslon, Caernarfon
LL54 7ST
☎ 01286 830242
www.inigojones.co.uk
The company was founded in 1870 to produce school writing slates and now produces a diverse range of slate goods for the home and garden. There is a self guided tour with introductory video presentation.

Penrhyn Castle (NT) (10m/17km)

Bangor
LL57 4HN
☎ 01248 371337
www.nationaltrust.org.uk
This neo-Norman castle, built in the 19th century for the wealthy Pennant family. The castle's interior has elaborate carvings, plasterwork and mock-Norman furniture. The Victorian kitchen and other servants' rooms, including scullery, larders and chef's sitting room, have been restored to how they were in the 1890s. The stable block houses an industrial railway museum..

Hotels and Dining

Try the local Tourist Information Centre, see Essential Contacts for details.

Something Special

Plas Dinas Country House (3m/4.5km)

Bontnewydd, Caernarfon,
Gwynedd
LL54 7YF
☎ 01286 830214
www.plasdinas.co.uk
Plas Dinas is a Grade II listed building dating back in parts to the mid 17th century.

Landmark Trust

The Bath Tower
Tower on the town wall by Menai Strait, sleeps 5

Ty'n Rhos Country House (7m/11km)

Seion, Llanddeiniolen,
nr. Caernarfon
LL55 3AE
☎ 01248 670 489
www.tynrhos.co.uk
Ty'n Rhos has 5 stars from the AA and the WTB, in addition it also has the coveted WTB Gold award. With the backdrop of Snowdonia and views across open farmland to Anglesey the hotel offers a relaxing luxury break.

The Celtic Royal Hotel

Bangor Street, Caernarfon
LL55 1AY
☎ 01286 674477
www.celtic-royal.co.uk
A stylish hotel in an 1841 listed building offers a fine dining restaurant and a leisure club including indoor heated swimming pool, sauna, jacuzzi and steam room, all in the centre of town.

Caer Menai

15 Church Street, Caernarfon
LL55 1SW
☎ 01286 672612
www.CaerMenai.co.uk
A WTB 4 star guest house within the old town walls.

Stones Bistro

4 Hole In The Wall Street
Caernarfon
LL55 1RF
☎ 01286 671152
Modern British food in a comfortable atmosphere.

Events

Bryn Terfel's Faenol Festival

August Bank Holiday

A steam engine at Caernarfon station on the Welsh Highland Railway

Essential Contacts

Tourist Information Centre
Oriel Pendeitsh, Castle Street
LL55 1ES
☎ 01286 672232
caernarfon.tic@gwynedd.gov.uk

Cardiff

Getting There

By Road
Cardiff is served by the M4 motorway.

By Rail
It is a mainline destination.

By Coach
National coaches go to Cardiff.

Background Briefing

Cardiff, the lively, cosmopolitan capital city of Wales, is a popular tourist destination with something for everyone: history, impressive buildings, shopping, nightlife, a vibrant waterfront in Cardiff Bay, beautiful parks and countryside nearby. The name Cardiff means fort on the (river) Taff and indeed the Romans did have a fort here but the town was founded by the Normans. It remained just a small town until the industrial revolution when the building of the Taff Vale Railway and the Merthyr Tydfil canal meant Cardiff was just a short journey away from the south Wales coalfield and Merthyr Tydfil, one of the worlds leading producers of iron. It became a major port exporting coal and iron all over the world.

The compact city centre can easily be explored on foot and a leaflet for the Cardiff Centenary Walk (from the Cardiff Visitor Centre) will guide you round the historic landmarks of the city. Alternatively the hop-on hop-off city sightseeing bus could be used.

Cathays Park to the north east of the castle houses the civic buildings and the museum and art gallery. The white Portland stone buildings erected in the early 20th century around this small park are of immense grandeur and certainly bear the hallmark of a capital city, despite having

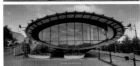

been built several decades before the official pronouncement in 1955. The castle, with its splendid neo-gothic interior, Norman keep and section of Roman wall and the Millennium Stadium, home of Welsh rugby, with its cantilevered walkways over the River Taff and its sliding roof, dominate the centre of the city.

The commercial heart of the city has many shopping opportunities from modern malls with all the leading stores you would expect to find in a modern city, to splendid Victorian and Edwardian arcades with small independent shops selling something a bit different. The traditional Victorian market houses a great variety of stalls selling everything from fresh food to gifts and greetings cards. There are many nationalities represented in the myriad of restaurants to suit all tastes and of course hotels from the cheap and cheerful to 5 star luxury. Entertainment venues ranges from the Edwardian New Theatre, the ultra modern Wales Millennium Centre and St David's Hall, the National Concert Hall of Wales, through to comedy clubs, live music venues and cinemas.

A 15 minute walk from the centre of the city down a long straight boulevard brings you to Cardiff Bay or of course you could hop on a bus. The bay has many imposing buildings with the old pier head building, a fine example of the brick maker's art, still a prominent feature. Alongside this building is the Oval basin, now converted into a piazza, with one huge, shiny, steel column in the centre and many smaller columns around the circumference, doubling as lights, the whole area having a feeling of enormous space. This sets the scene for the use of the waterfront as a sculpture park; look out for the great ring, the life-size couple and child and the two figures in a bath, all by the Mermaid Quay. Adjacent to the Oval is the Millennium Centre and nearby Y Senedd, home of the Welsh Assembly, two impressive modern buildings both open to the public. It's also worth taking a short walk past Lightship 2000, along Britannia Quay, to view the strange terra cotta figures. Mermaid Quay has a large range of restaurants, bars and shops and the nearby Red Dragon Centre is a modern exciting, entertainment complex, with a variety of venues and restaurants with cuisine from all parts of the globe.

There is a huge freshwater lake created by the building of the Cardiff Bay Barrage where you can find cruises, sailing and watersports with many events organised by the Harbour Authority.

There is the yellow water bus running between the waterfront and the end of the barrage at Penarth. Alternatively the Cardiff Road Train will take you past all the sights of Cardiff Bay plus the working docks (which are closed to the public) and across the barrage.

For some respite from the hustle and bustle of a busy city there are

Above: Cardiff Castle
Opposite page top: Urban sculpture named "people like us", Cardiff Bay
Opposite page bottom: Cardiff Bay Visitor Centre, Britannia Quay

several parks to enjoy or you could take a trip to Flat Holm Island, a nature reserve in the Bristol Channel 5 miles south of Cardiff. A boat runs to the island from Cardiff Bay from March to October.

Places to visit

Cardiff Castle

Castle Street, Cardiff
CF10 3RB
☎ 029 2087 8100
www.cardiffcastle.com

In the centre of the city Cardiff Castle with a history which spans nearly 2000 years is an interesting visit. It has been a Roman garrison, a Norman stronghold and in Victorian times its apartments were created by eccentric architect William Burgess for the 3rd Marquess of Bute in a neo-gothic style. The rooms are filled with intricate stained glass, ornate fireplaces, gilded ceilings, and carved and painted animals throughout.

In the grounds are the museum of the Royal Regiment of Wales and the Norman Keep.

National Museum Wales

Cathays Park, Cardiff
CF10 3NP
☎ 029 2039 7951
www.museumwales.ac.uk

Museum and art gallery with extensive collections including Archaeology, Biology, Geology, Industry and Social History plus much more. The art gallery has the largest collection of impressionist paintings outside Paris.

Millennium Stadium

A☎ 02920 822228
www.millenniumstadium.com

The home of Welsh Rugby, the Millennium Stadium stages many events from rugby and football to music and concerts, tours of the stadium are available most days.

Norwegian Church

Norwegian Church Arts Centre, Harbour Drive, Cardiff Bay
CF10 4PA
☎ 02920 454899
www.norwegianchurchcardiff.co.uk

The Norwegian Church, an iconic building in the Bay, was built in 1868 to provide for the many Norwegian merchant seamen that passed through the port of Cardiff. It is now a busy arts centre with exhibitions, concerts and other events throughout the year.

Wales Millennium Centre

Bute Place, Cardiff
CF10 5AL
☎ 02920 636400
www.wmc.org.uk

The Centre, opened in 2004, is an impressive building containing two theatres and a smaller hall, shops, bars and restaurants, and seven resident Welsh arts organisations. It has an extensive programme of events including musicals, choirs, opera and ballet to music and comedy to suit all tastes. There is a guided tour of the building and there is usually something going on throughout the day.

Y Senedd/ home of the Welsh Assembly Government

The National Assembly for Wales, Cardiff Bay, Cardiff,
CF99 1NA
www.assemblywales.org

A spectacular modern building open to the public.

Llandaff Cathedral (2m/4km)

Llandaff, Cardiff
CF5 2YF

The ancient cathedral city of Llandaff is now a peaceful village complete with village green and tea rooms. Stop at Llandaff Cathedral, built on a site that has had a church since the 6th century, and see the aluminium statue of Christ in Majesty by Sir Jacob Epstein.

Welsh Assembly Building, Cardiff Bay

Wales Millennium Centre and Pierhead Building, Cardiff Bay

Llandaff Cathedral at the city within a city

Attractions Nearby

Castell Coch (Cadw) and Forest Fawr (Forestry Commission) (5.5m/9km)
Tongwynlais, Cardiff
☎ 029 2050 0200
www.castellcoch.info
Castell Coch, another Victorian gothic fairytale castle designed by William Burgess for the 3rd Marquess of Bute, is set in Forest Fawr, a few miles to the north of the city. Forest Fawr is an ancient beech wood and Site of Special Scientific Interest with rare plants and butterflies. The carpets of bluebells and anemones in the spring are a spectacular sight, a peaceful haven after the bustling city.

St Fagans: National History Museum (4.5m/7km)
St Fagans, Cardiff
CF5 6XB
☎ 029 20573500
www.museumwales.ac.uk/en/stfagans
Outdoor museum of Welsh life, set in the grounds of a 16th century manor house, St Fagans Castle. It has many old buildings, houses, a chapel, a farm and school re-erected on site. It also has galleries of costume, daily life and special exhibitions, a must see for those interested in Welsh traditions and how life was in the past.

Hotels and Dining
Try the local Tourist Information Centre, see Essential Contacts for details.

Something Special

St David's Hotel & Spa
Havannah Street, Cardiff Bay
CF10 5SD
☎ 02920 454045
www.StDavidsHotelCardiff.co.uk
A modern 5 star hotel on the waterfront in Cardiff Bay with an award winning restaurant.

The Royal Hotel
10 St Mary Street, Cardiff
CF10 1DW
☎ 02920 550750
www.theroyalhotelcardiff.com
A boutique style hotel adjacent to the Millennium Stadium in the city centre.

Lincoln House Private Hotel
118-120 Cathedral Road
Cardiff
CF11 9LQ
☎ 02920 395558
www.lincolnhotel.co.uk
A Victorian townhouse, restored to retain its character whilst providing modern comfort.

The Big Sleep Hotel
Bute Terrace, Cardiff
CF10 2FE
☎ 02920 636363
www.thebigsleephotel.com
An ultra modern stylish hotel with light airy rooms and wonderful views. It is conveniently situated less than 10 minutes walk from the central railway station.

Armless Dragon
97 Wyeverne Road, Cathays, Cardiff, Wales
☎ 02920 382357
Contemporary Welsh Cuisine at its best.

Strada – Cardiff
24 Mermaid Quay
Cardiff Bay
CF10 5BZ
☎ 02920 482112
An Italian restaurant on the water front with alfresco dining.

Essential Contacts

Cardiff Visitor Centre
The Old Library, The Hayes
Cardiff
CF10 1WE
☎ 08701 211258

Cardiff Harbour Authority
Queen Alexandra House
Cargo Road, Cardiff Bay
Cardiff
CF10 4LY
☎ 02920 877900
www.cardiffharbour.com
The Harbour Authority has a calendar of local, national and international water and land based events.

Cardiff Bay Visitor Centre
Harbour Drive, Cardiff Bay
CF10 4PA
☎ 02920 463833
www.visitcardiffbay.info

The Red Dragon Centre
Hemingway Road, Leisure Village, Cardiff
CF10 4JY
☎ 02920 256261
www.thereddragoncentre.co.uk

Chepstow, Monmouthshire

Getting There

By Road
M4 or M5 then M48 over Severn Bridge (toll).

By Rail
Chepstow is on the branch line between Newport and Cheltenham.

By Coach
There is a national coach service to Chepstow.

Background Briefing

The River Wye flows into the Severn Estuary at Chepstow, on the border between England and Wales. With its spectacular castle high on the cliffs above the River Wye, impressive 13th century town walls and its twisting, mediaeval streets there are plenty reminders of its historic past. The old town walls were built not as a defence but as a means of controlling entry to the town and the 15th century town gate, now used as the town council offices, is on the site of the original gate and portcullis. Three walking trails will guide you round the town. The most popular is the town centre trail, the route of which is within the town wall. There is a more extensive town trail and a riverside trail for the less energetic. All routes start and finish at the Castle Car Park.

For atmosphere and excitement a day at the races is hard to beat and Chepstow racecourse enjoys an unrivalled setting above the town in Piercefield Park. It has meetings throughout the year both on the flat and over jumps.

Chepstow is at the end of two long distance walks; Offa's Dyke path which runs roughly along the border of Wales and England from Prestatyn on the north coast and the Wye Valley walk which starts at the source of the Wye on Plynlimon. For the energetic it is possible to walk to nearby Tintern Abbey, a must see destination with its imposing ruins in an idyllic setting, using the two paths. A leaflet is available from the Tourist Information Office.

Places to visit

Chepstow Castle (Cadw)
Bridge Street
NP16 5EY
☎ 01291 624065
www.Cadw.wales.gov.uk/default.asp?id=245

Perched on limestone cliffs above the River Wye, Chepstow castle is one the earliest to be built of stone, the Normans building the stone keep in 1067. It was built to guard the main river crossing from southern England into Wales.

Chepstow Museum
Gwy House, Bridge Street
NP16 5EZ
☎ 01291 625981

Across the road from the castle, the museum is housed in an impressive 18th century house with an interesting history. The museum displays the town's past as a port and market town. There are exhibits about the wine and timber trades plus ship building and salmon fishing. There is a collection of 18th and 19th century prints, drawings and paintings of Chepstow and the Wye Valley.

The Parish and Priory Church of St Mary
Church Street

The Norman Priory of Chepstow was built at the same time as the keep of Chepstow Castle. The original west front and nave of the church can still be seen and it has a striking Norman arch at the west entrance.

Right: The Towngate; Right top: Chepstow Castle; Right bottom: Tintern Abbey

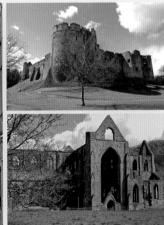

Attractions Nearby

Tintern Abbey (Cadw) (5m/8km)

Tintern, Chepstow

NP16 6SE

☎ 01291 689251

Set on a beautiful site in the wooded Wye Valley, Tintern Abbey is an imposing, much photographed ruin. Originally founded in 1131 for Cistercian monks it was rebuilt in the 13th century and although it is without roof or windows it remains an impressive building.

Caldicot Castle and Country Park (5m/8km)

Church Road, Caldicot.

NP26 4HU

☎ 01291 420241

www.caldicotcastle.co.uk

Caldicot is a picturesque castle set in a country park with gardens and woodland. Founded by the Normans its long history is explained by the audio tour available for visitors. There is a tearoom and gift shop plus tourist information. It is open from March to October.

Caerwent/Venta Silurum Roman town (5m/8km)

Caldicot

The extensive remains of this Roman town include a complete circuit of the town walls, in places still over sixteen feet (five metres) high, the foundations of several Roman houses and shops and a small Romano-Celtic temple.

Dewstow Gardens (6m/10km)

Caerwent, Monmouthshire

NP26 5AH

☎ 01291 430444

www.dewstow.com

Open late March to mid October

The Hidden Gardens and Grottoes of Dewstow were built around 1895 and included caves, grottoes, tunnels, water features and ferneries, which were all buried for over 50 years and rediscovered in 2000. They are now being restored and much of the garden has been replanted.

Veddw House Gardens (5m/8km)

Veddw House, Devauden, Monmouthshire

NP16 6PH

☎ 01291 650836

www.veddw.co.uk

Open Sundays in summer.

If you are in the Wye Valley on a Sunday afternoon, not to be missed is this impressive modern privately owned garden with ornamental gardens and woodland.

Hotels and Dining

Try the local Tourist Information Centre, see Essential Contacts for details.

Something Special

Marriott St Pierre Hotel and Country Club

St Pierre Park

Chepstow

NP16 6YA

☎ 01291 625261

The St Pierre is a 14th century manor house set in 400 acres of parkland with every amenity you would expect in a modern hotel. The facilities include two 18-hole golf courses, 13 bay floodlit driving range, large indoor swimming pool, sauna, spa bath, steam room, fully equipped gym and health and beauty suite.

The Beaufort Hotel

Beaufort Square, Chepstow

Gwent

NP16 5EP

☎ 01291 622497

www.beauforthotelchepstow.com

The family run Beaufort Hotel offers modern facilities in this 16th century former coaching inn. The award winning restaurant uses locally sourced produce and features traditional British and international dishes.

Castle View Hotel

16 Bridge Street, Chepstow

NP16 5EZ

☎ 01291 620349

www.hotelchepstow.co.uk

This small hotel has wonderful views of the castle.

Afon Gwy Restaurant with rooms

28 Bridge Street, Chepstow

NP16 5EZ

☎ 01291 620158

www.afongwy.co.uk

The restaurant built around 1735 has lovely views of the castle and the old Wye Bridge. It offers a modern British cuisine in a brasserie style menu.

Events

Chepstow Festival

July

Two Rivers Folk Festival

July

Essential Contacts

Chepstow Tourist Information Centre

Castle Car Park

Bridge Street

NP16 5EY

☎ 01291 623772

Chepstow Race Course

St. Lawrence Rd, Chepstow

NP16 6BE

☎ 01291 622260

www.chepstow-racecourse.co.uk

Getting There

By Road

Conwy is situated just off the A55 Chester to Holyhead road.

By Rail

Conwy station lies in the centre of town and is served by trains on the Chester to Holyhead line.

By Coach

Coach to Llandudno then onward by local bus.

Background Briefing

Conwy is a small town of immense charm, rich in historical interest and set in an incredibly beautiful landscape on the North Wales coast.

Approach Conwy from the east and you sense immediately you are arriving at a special place: to the right are the sparkling waters of the Conwy estuary, with a myriad of small boats bobbing at anchor; ahead is the massive bulk of the castle, with its lofty battlements and the compact old town enclosed within high medieval walls, while in the background is a backdrop of towering mountains.

The obvious starting point for a first visit to Conwy has to be the castle, a structure which dominates the town and attracts visitors like a magnet; a World Heritage Site, this is possibly the best example of a medieval castle in Wales. Closely linked to the castle, both physically and historically, are the town walls; it is possible to walk along the top of most of the circuit and it gives an exhilarating high level view over the rooftops, an experience not to be missed.

Moving forward in time, the 16th century saw the building of the magnificent town house of Plas Mawr by a wealthy local merchant. This fine old house has been painstakingly restored to its Elizabethan grandeur and an audio tour explains about the restoration of the building and life in the Tudor and Stuart periods. If you've still not had your fill of historical buildings Aberconwy House, a smaller but older house, is well worth a visit.

Conwy is a great place for exploring on foot. Wander along the quayside, enjoying the views over the estuary and maybe taking a look at the quirky "smallest house" or visiting the Mussel Museum. Alternatively browse through the many independent small shops,

Above: Conwy quay

Bottom left: Llewelyn the Great in Lancaster Square; **Middle:** Aberconwy House; **Right:** The smallest House in Gt. Britain

Places to visit

Conwy Castle (Cadw)

LL32 8AY

☎ 01492 592358

A triumph of medieval military engineering this magnificent stone edifice has proved remarkably resilient to the passage of time over the seven centuries since it was built. It still stands sentinel over the River Conwy as it has since it was built by Edward I to further his strategy to subdue the local inhabitants; today it can be regarded as a thing of beauty, and one that gives a fascinating insight into the turbulent times of the 13th century in Wales.

Plas Mawr (Cadw)

High Street

LL32 8DE

☎ 01492 580167

This imposing 16th century town house dominates Conwy High Street. Built by a wealthy merchant and courtier, Robert Wynn, the house features some magnificent plasterwork and fine carpentry, all carefully restored by Cadw.

Conwy Butterfly Jungle

Bodlondeb Park

LL32 8DU

☎ 01492 593149

www.conwy-butterfly.co.uk

Aberconwy House (NT)

Castle Street

LL32 8AY

(01492 592246

Built in the 14th century this merchant's house is said to be the oldest in Wales. An audio-visual tour explains how the house developed over 600 years and the rooms are furnished to show the changes over the centuries.

looking out for the colourful statue of Llewelyn ap Iowerth in Lancaster Square. Call in at the Royal Cambrian Academy of Art to view the latest exhibition, take a look at Telford's elegant suspension bridge, built to visually complement the castle, or pause for refreshment at the small coffee shop located within one of the towers of the town walls overlooking the quay. Venturing slightly further afield a level walk along the Cob to Deganwy or a stiff but short climb up Conwy Mountain are recommended. When you're tired of walking a boat trip from the Quay will rest the feet while giving a different viewpoint on the scenery.

Top: Telford's suspension bridge and the castle wall; Middle: The Castle; Bottom: Plas Mawr; Opposite page: Bodnant Gardens (NT)

Royal Academy of Art
Crown Lane
LL32 8AN
☎ 01492 593413
www.rcaconwy.org

Pinewood Riding Stables
Sychnant Pass Road
LL32 8BZ
☎ 01492 592256
Horse rides on Conwy Mountain and nearby hills for novices and experienced riders.

Conwy Water Gardens (4m/7km)
Glyn Isa, Rowen
LL32 8TP
☎ 01492 650063
Coarse fishing on three lakes in a beautiful valley.

Attractions Nearby

RSPB Conwy Reserve (1m/1.6 km)
Llandudno Junction
☎ 01492 584091
Great views and lots of interesting birds on this estuarine reserve.

Bodnant Gardens (NT) (5.5m/9km)
Tal-y-Cafn
LL28 5RE
☎ 01492 650460
www.bodnantgardens.co.uk
Beautifully situated overlooking the Conwy Valley, these 80 acre

gardens with terraces, lawns and a wooded dell are often a riot of colour; if visiting in June look out for the famous laburnum arch.

Aber Falls (9.5m/15km)
Abergwyngregyn
A spectacular sight after heavy rain the 115ft/35m cascade is reached by a pleasant easy walk through woods in a steep sided valley.

Hotels and Dining
Try the local Tourist Information Centre, see Essential Contacts for details.

Something Special

Castle Hotel
High Street
LL32 8DB
☎ 01492 582800
www.castlewales.co.uk
Old coaching house in centre of town, expanded and modernised to provide all modern amenities.

Castlebank Hotel
Mount Pleasant
LL32 8NY
☎ 01492 593888
www.castlebankhotel.co.uk
Victorian house, standing in its own grounds just outside the town walls, converted into a friendly, family run hotel; some of the rooms have superb views over the Conwy estuary.

Bryn Guest House
Sychnant Pass Road
LL32 8NS
☎ 01492 592449
www.bryn.org.uk
Comfortable B+B in Victorian house with gardens bordering the medieval town walls.

Sychnant Pass House
Sychnant Pass Road
LL32 8BJ
☎ 01492 596868
www.sychnant-pass-house

Set in open country overlooking the town this country house hotel's facilities include indoor pool, hot tub and gymnasium.

Tyr y Coed Country House
Rowen
LL32 8TP
☎ 01492 650219
www.tirycoed.com
Relaxation is the watchword at this elegant small hotel in one of the most attractive villages in North Wales.

Alfredo's Restaurant
Lancaster Square
LL32 8DA
☎ 01492 592381

Llewelyn's Restaurant
High Street
LL32 8DB
☎ 01492 592232

The Groes Inn (3m/5km)
LL32 8TN
☎ 01492 650545
www.groesinn.com
A choice of formal or informal dining at this country inn, the first licensed house in Wales.

The Groes has a couple of apartments, one nearby and one in Conwy, of exceptional quality, as well as accommodation at the inn.

Events

Walking Week

Bluegrass Festival

Classic Music Festival

Honey Fair

Conwy Feast

Fishguard, Pembrokeshire

Getting There

By Road
A40 from Carmarthen or A487 from Cardigan.

By Rail
Fishguard Harbour (limited service) or Haverfordwest, then onward by local bus.

By Coach
Limited service to Haverfordwest.

Lower Fishguard

Background Briefing

The small town in north Pembrokeshire known as Fishguard in English or Abergwaun in Welsh is a town in three parts: Lower Town with the old harbour; Fishguard town; and Goodwick, site of the new harbour.

As may be inferred from the English name for the town the principal occupation was once fishing but Lower Town, a picturesque old harbour with quaint quayside cottages is now used mainly by leisure craft. It's worth visiting the Old Fort, a short walk away on Castle Point, a good viewpoint with some splendid old cannons.

The main road from Cardigan snakes its way through the narrow streets of Lower Town, crosses the river Gwaun before leaping up the steep cliff side to emerge at the square in Fishguard town. Here you will find all manner of shops, cafes and ancient inns. The recently refurbished Town Hall houses the Tourist Information Centre, library and indoor market. It's also the place to see the 'Last Invasion Tapestry' which illustrates, in the style of the Bayeux Tapestry, the story of the abortive attempt by a French force to invade the country in 1797. The Royal Oak Inn, also on the square, is where the French formally surrendered.

The Marine Walk leads from the town around the headland towards Goodwick; there are fine views over the harbour, with information boards adding to the interest. The path drops down to the Parrog, with a half mile long promenade alongside Goodwick Sands leading to the new harbour at Goodwick. From here Stena Line ferries sail twice a day to Rosslare Harbour in southern Ireland, augmented in summer by a fast catamaran service which can reach Rosslare in 1½ hours. A striking new building on the Parrog is home to Ocean Lab where in addition to a tourist information centre and cafe you will find Ocean Quest, a child friendly exhibition of marine life.

Pembrokeshire is renowned for its coastal path and the section around Fishguard and neighbouring Newport is one of the best. Highly recommended is the coast

Above left: Pwll Deri Youth Hostel on the coastal path; **Right:** Sign on the Royal Oak Inn

walk from Goodwick to Pwll Deri. The path climbs steeply from the harbour before levelling out and following the indented rocky shoreline past Carregwastad Point, the site of the French landing, with its memorial stone, to rugged windswept Strumble Head and its lighthouse. The route now heads south towards the beautiful rocky bay of Pwll Deri, overlooked by the craggy summit of Garn Fawr. The best time to do this walk is undoubtedly May or June when the wild flowers are at their best. Along the path you will see many different varieties of flower, varying with subtle changes in soil, moisture, shade and aspect; pink thrift, brilliant white oxeye daisy, bluebell, delicate yellow primrose, red and white campion, purple vetch. The abundance and variety of this floral extravaganza is truly amazing, with the symphony of colour reaching its crescendo on the steep slopes above Pwll Deri; pause for a while to enjoy, before taking the quiet byway to Trefasser Cross for the bus back to Fishguard.

It's easy to leave the car behind in this area in the summer months. From May to September the Coast-bus service runs two useful routes passing through Fishguard. The Strumble Shuttle runs between Fishguard and St David's, calling at Strumble Head, Trefasser Cross and Tregwynt. The Poppet Rocket serves Dinas, Newport and Nefyn on its way to Cardigan.

Places to visit

Ocean Lab
Goodwick
SA64 0DE
☎ 01348 872037
Child friendly exhibition of marine life in a modern building on the sea front with café and soft play area.

Above left: Strumble Head Lighthouse; **Above right:** Nolton Haven

Above: The Castle, Newport

Above: Display at Garn post office

Attractions Nearby

Melin Tregwynt (6m/10km)
Castlemorris
SA62 5UX
☎ 01348 891644
www.melintregwynt
This flourishing, long established family business, designs and manufactures woollen clothing in a historic mill deep in the Pembrokeshire countryside. Combining traditional fabric with innovative designs its products can be found in stores around the world. Visit the mill to see the weaving process taking place, browse the shop containing many of the products made on site and relax with a drink in the coffee shop.

Castell Henllys Iron Age Fort (11m/18km)
Meline, Crymych
SA41 3UT
☎ 01239 891319
www.castellhenllys.com
See how our ancestors lived at this award winning reconstructed hill fort. Beautifully located and set in 30 acres of woodland and river meadows the site interprets archaeological finds in a novel way.

Pentre Ifan Burial Chamber (Cadw) (9.5m/15km)
Pentre Ifan, near Newport
www.Cadw.wales.gov.uk
Probably the most visited of all the many prehistoric monuments in Wales and it's easy to see why. First there's the spectacular setting in open countryside with views of surrounding hills and out to sea. Then there's the monument itself; marvel at the huge capstone delicately poised on three uprights and wonder how they got it up there with only the most basic of tools. Take a moment to contemplate how man's existence has changed over the millennia since this tomb was constructed.

Dinas Head (4.5m/7km)
Walk the circular route around the headland or laze on the sand on one of the two sandy coves.

Newport (7m/11.5km)
Climb to the summit of rocky Carn Ingli or take it easy on the broad sands of Newport beach.

Hotels and Dining
Try the local Tourist Information Centre, see Essential Contacts for details.

Gellifawr Hotel (5.5m/9km)
Pontfaen
SA65 9TX
☎ 01239 820343
www.gellifawr.co.uk
Located in the breathtakingly beautiful Gwaun Valley. Enjoy a relaxing stay at this friendly, family run hotel.

Ferryboat Inn
Manor Wat, Dyffryn
Goodwick
SA64 0AE
☎ 01348 874747
www.ferryboatinn.co.uk
Simple modern décor in a recently refurbished four star inn. Enjoy locally sourced food in a traditional inn setting.

Seaview Hotel
The Seafront
SA65 9PL
☎ 01348 874282
www.seaviewhotel.co.uk
Family run hotel which as the name suggests has fine views out to sea.

Plaindealings B+B
Towerhill
SA65 9LA
☎ 01348 873655
Five star rated guest house in secluded position overlooking Lower Town. No children.

Bar 5 Restaurant
5 Main Street
SA65 9HA
☎ 01348 875050
Contemporary styling on three floors with a terrace giving views over the old harbour.

Three Main Street
3 Main Street
SA 65 9HG
☎ 01348 871845
An emphasis on local sourcing at this elegant Georgian town house restaurant.

Newport Links Hotel (10m/16km)
Golf Course Road, Newport
SA42 0NR
☎ 01239 820244
Comfortable small hotel overlooking Newport Bay. Golfing enthusiasts will want to try out the 80 year old links course but non golfers are just as welcome.

Events

Fishguard International Music Festival

Fishguard Folk Festival

Essential Contacts

Fishguard Town TIC
The Town Hall, The Square
SA65 9HA
☎ 01348 776636

Fishguard Harbour TIC
Ocean Lab, The Parrog
SA64 0DE
☎ 01348 874737

Theatr Gwaun
West Street
SA65 9AD
☎ 01348 873421
A 180 seat venue showing a varied programme of film and some live shows.

Getting There

By Road

At M4 Junction 42 take the A483 to Swansea. From Swansea take the A4118 which runs the length of the peninsula.

By Rail

Rail to Swansea then onward by local bus.

By Coach

Coach to Swansea then onward by local bus.

Above: Rhossili Downs in the Gower peninsula

Flowers Gower peninsula

Background Briefing

The Gower Peninsula juts out into the sea to the west of the city of Swansea. The first Area of Outstanding Natural Beauty to be so designated in the UK this tract of beautiful unspoilt countryside measures some 16m/25km long by 7m/11km wide.

Gower's fame is rooted in its glorious beaches. The largest number of these is to be found on the south coast; Langland, Caswell and Oxwich Bays all have popular family beaches, with miles of golden sand and safe bathing. Also on the south coast are the tiny secluded Pwll Du and the much lauded Three Cliffs Bay, a beautiful beach reached only on foot. On the west coast lies Rossili Bay, with its 3m/5km of sand stretching up to the islet of Burry Holm. The northern stretch of the bay is known as Llangennith Beach and is much favoured by surfers. There is little in the way of beaches

Above: Coasteering and abseiling on the Gower peninsula

on the northern shore but it is worth visiting Llanrhidian or Pen Clawdd to experience the sleepy villages and the eerie marshlands with their grazing sheep and ponies.

There's also plenty to do away from the beach. Walkers can enjoy a walk on the cliff tops such as the five mile route on the wild craggy cliffs between Port Eynon and Rhossili. Inland lies Cefn Bryn, a ridge of Old Red Sandstone rising to 610ft/186m; this is an area of open moorland, bare and bleak, with many prehistoric monuments, and a good place for walks.

Another popular walk is to Rhossili Down, the highest point on Gower overlooking the sweep of Rhossili Bay. Nature lovers have a choice of 19 nature reserves to choose from. They vary from large to very small and cover many habitats including woodland, marshland, meadow, grassland and heath. Pony trekking is a popular activity on the peninsula and riders can head to Parc-le-Breos to pick up a mount.

A more intangible appeal to visitors to Gower is the sense of otherworldliness; the narrow winding roads slowing down the pace of life; the peaceful unspoilt villages with timeless allure. But if the peace and quiet gets too much there's always Swansea and its many attractions just a short step away.

Places to visit

Gower Heritage Centre
Parkmill
SA3 2EH
☎ 01792 371206
www.gowerheritagecentre.co.uk
A museum of rural life set in a 12th century water mill. Craft shops, animal farm and play areas. Fun for all the family.

Worm's Head
When viewed from a distance, and using a little imagination, it's not difficult to see why the Vikings thought this spit of land at the very western tip of Gower looked like a sea serpent and gave it their name for such a mythical creature. It's certainly a very special place and attracts thousands of visitors every year. The serpent's body is a long grassy hill separated from the mainland by rocks covered by the high tide; the craggy pinnacle of the head is connected to the body by a natural arch. The adventurous will be tempted to explore, and it is possible to make your way to the very tip of the headland; but be aware that the crossing can only be made for 2½ hours each side of low water and it's likely to be a very uncomfortable experience if you find yourself stranded.

Hotels and Dining
Try the local Tourist Information Centre, see Essential Contacts for details.

Something Special

Parc-le-Breos House
Parkmill
SA3 2HA
☎ 01792 371636
www.parclebreos.co.uk
Escape from the pressures of modern life at this 19th century hunting lodge set in 70 acres of parkland and close to the wonderful Three Cliffs Bay. You can wander the extensive gardens, take tea on the terrace or try some fishing in the trout ponds. The guest house also operates as a pony trekking centre.

Fairyhill
Reynoldston
SA3 1BS
☎ 01792 390139
www.fairyhill.net
Five star country house hotel with award winning restaurant in 24 acres of parkland.

Littlehaven Guest House
Oxwich
SA3 1LS
☎ 01792 390940
www.littlehavenoxwich.co.uk
Comfortable guest house close to Oxwich beach with garden and outdoor heated swimming pool.

Welcome to Town
Llanrhidian
SA3 1EH
☎ 01792 390015
www.thewelcometotown.co.uk
Award winning country bistro in a north Gower village.

Worm's Head Hotel
Rhossili
SA3 1PP
☎ 01792 390512
www.thewormshead.co.uk
Not only good food but stunning views on offer at this cliff top hotel.

Oxwich Bay Hotel
Oxwich Bay
SA3 1LS
☎ 01792 390329
www.oxwichbayhotel.co.uk
Hotel and restaurant in wonderful location overlooking the beach.

Events

Gower Walking Festival

Essential Contacts

Swansea Tourist Information Centre
☎ 01792 468321

Mumbles Tourist Information Centre
☎ 01792 361302

Gower Coast Adventures
150 Pennard Drive, Southgate
Swansea
SA3 2DR
☎ 01792 297157
www.gowercoastadventures.co.uk
Thrill a minute boat trips from Port Eynon beach in rigid hulled inflatables.

Above: Viewpoint on the Gower peninsula

Getting There

By Road

Haverfordwest is on the A40 between Fishguard and Carmarthen.

By Rail

There is a 2 hourly service from London to Haverfordwest.

By Coach

National coaches have a limited service to Haverfordwest.

Above: Gateholm Island with Skokholm beyond, near Marloes

Background Briefing

Haverfordwest, the county town of Pembrokeshire, makes a good base for exploring the delights of west Pembrokeshire, renowned for its exceptional coastline. The town has many historic buildings, including Georgian buildings built during one of its periods of prosperity, a castle, and four parish churches. The castle was built in the 12th century and the town museum is situated within its walls. The remains of the old Augustinian priory with its cloister garden can be seen on the outskirts of town.

It is a busy town with lots of shops, restaurants, accommodation and pubs for the visitor to choose from. The town was once a thriving port and the converted quay area also has many places to eat to suit all pockets. There are riverside and country walks from the centre of town and the Celtic Trail cycle route, part of Sustrans route 4, passes through the town.

St Brides Bay is the area of the Pembrokeshire Coast National Park between the headlands of St Davids and Marloes: it is a broad sweep of exceptional coastline facing the Atlantic Ocean. If you want quiet sandy beaches, stunning coastal scenery and wildlife in abundance this is definitely the area to visit.

The many beaches vary from small and secluded to the enormous Blue Flag beach at Newgale, with its 2m/3km of sand and many water sport activities.

The Pembrokeshire Coast Path runs all the way round St Brides Bay and using the Puffin Shuttle bus the visitor does not have to devise a circular walk. The path is a delight to walk, particularly in the late spring, with its spectacular scenery, cliff tops carpeted with wild flowers and beautiful white beaches. There are colonies of seabirds nesting along the cliffs, and seal, porpoises and dolphin can all be seen swimming offshore.

Places to visit

Haverfordwest Town Museum

Castle House, Haverfordwest
SA61 2EF
☎ 01437 763087
www.haverfordwest-town-museum.org.uk
Situated within the Castle wall and previously the old prison governor's house the town museum has local history and art exhibits.

Skomer and Skokholm Islands

The Wildlife Trust of South and West Wales
☎ 01656 724100
www.welshwildlife.org

Skomer Island is a national nature reserve managed by the Wildlife Trust of South and West Wales. It has impressive scenery with carpets of wild flowers in late spring and early summer; the bluebells are particularly spectacular. It is a bird watchers' paradise with over ten thousand puffins and a hundred thousand Manx shearwaters breeding in the burrows on the island, plus guillemots, razorbills and fulmars nesting on the cliffs. It is home to the unique Skomer vole and grey seals can be seen year round. Skokholm Island is somewhat different with its old red sandstone cliffs topped by a plateau of rabbit maintained vegetation. It too has many breeding seabirds including Manx shearwaters, storm petrels, puffins, razorbills and guillemots. It is an SSSI and part of the Skomer and Skokholm Special Protection Area.

Both islands can be visited by boat from Martins Haven near Marloes but visits to Skokholm are very limited and need to be booked in advance at:

Island Bookings ☎ 01239 621600 or ☎ 01239 621212

Skomer can be visited from Tuesday to Sunday from the beginning of April to the end of October. There is no advance booking; it is first come first served from Martins Haven.

Top: Little Haven near Broad Haven
Bottom: A Puffin

Attractions Nearby

Torch Theatre (7.5 m/12km)
St. Peters Road, Milford Haven
SA73 2BU
☎ 01646 695267
www.torchtheatre.co.uk
The Torch Theatre, with its own repertory company, provides Pembrokeshire with a variety of entertainment including comedy, drama, children's shows, dance, opera and musicals. Latest film releases are also shown and in the gallery are exhibitions of paintings, photographs, ceramics, crafts and installations by local amateur and professional artists. The theatre has its own cafe and bar.

Pembroke Castle (11m/18km)
Pembroke
SA71 4LA
☎ 01646 684585
www.pembroke-castle.co.uk
Set on the river bank the castle is mostly intact and has exhibitions illustrating its medieval life. It is famous as the birth place of Henry Tudor, later to become Henry VII.

Pembrokeshire Motor Museum (5m/8km)
Keeston, Haverfordwest
SA62 6EJ
www.pembsmotormuseum.co.uk
The museum has over 40 exhibits ranging from a veteran 1906 Rover to the modern classic 1969/70 Jaguar "E" type series II.

Hotels and Dining
Try the local Tourist Information Centre, see Essential Contacts for details.

The County Hotel
Salutation Square, Haverfordwest
SA61 2NB
☎ 01437 762144
www.county-hotel.com
A WTB 4 star hotel dating from 1842, which has been sympathetically refurbished by its present owners to retain its character. The restaurant uses fresh local produce.

Pembroke House Hotel
6/7 Spring Gardens, Barn Street
Haverfordwest
SA61 2EJ
☎ 01437 779622
www.pembrokehousehotel.com
The hotel is set in a quiet part of Haverfordwest.

East Hook Farmhouse
Portfield Gate, Haverfordwest
SA62 3LN
☎ 01437 762211
www.easthookfarmhouse.co.uk
3m/5km west of Haverfordwest towards Broadhaven the farm offers WTB 4 star B&B accommodation.

Wolfscastle Country Hotel
Wolfscastle, Haverfordwest
SA62 5LZ
☎ 01437 741225
A former vicarage with a warm and welcoming atmosphere, the hotel is AA & WTB 3 star and has an AA rosette and Taste of Wales award for its restaurant.

Stone Hall Mansion
Welsh Hook, Haverfordwest
SA62 5NS
☎ 01348 840212
www.stonehall-mansion.co.uk
The restaurant is Good Food Guide recommended. French country cuisine using local ingredients.

Landmark Trust
West Blockhouse, Dale
Built in 1857, guarding entrance to Milford Haven, sleeps up to 8.

Events

Haverfordwest Farmers Market
Held fortnightly.

Essential Contacts

Haverfordwest Tourist Information Centre
19 Old Bridge Street, Haverfordwest
SA61 2EZ
☎ 01437 763110

Mikes Bikes
17 Prendergast, Haverfordwest
SA61 2PE
☎ 01437 760068
www.mikes-bikes.co.uk
Cycle hire.

Newsurf
Newgale, Haverfordwest
SA62 6AS
☎ 01437 721398
www.newsurf.co.uk
Surfing Instruction.

Big Blue Experience
Newsurf, Newgale
SA62 6AS
☎ 07816 169359
www.bigbluekitesurfing.com
Kite Surfing and Kite Boarding.

Buses
For details of buses along the coast path
www.pembrokeshire.gov.uk/coastbus

Hay-on-Wye, Powys

Getting There

By Road
Just off the A438 Hereford to Brecon road.

By Rail
Train to Hereford then onward by local bus.

By Coach
Coach to Hereford then onward by local bus

Above: Hay Castle and Bookshop

Background Briefing

Hay-on-Wye sits at the north-east tip of the Brecon Beacons National Park, nudging the Herefordshire border. Here the River Wye slows and broadens as it meanders towards Hereford. To the south the skyline is dominated by the escarpment of the Black Mountains, to the north lie the rolling hills of mid-Wales.

A small town with a history traceable back to Norman times it has been for many centuries a busy market town serving the surrounding district and a flourishing outdoor market is still held here today, every Thursday in the Buttermarket and Memorial Square. However, since the 1960s the commercial activity of the town has increasingly been dominated by the second hand book trade. There are now over thirty bookshops in Hay, with shelves often spilling out onto the street, and there are reckoned to be over a million books for sale covering every subject imaginable; a veritable paradise for bibliophiles! A visitor wandering through the narrow streets will soon appreciate the designation 'Town of Books' and even non aficionados will be drawn to sample the wares.

But there is much more to Hay than its bookshops. The town is a major centre for outdoor activities

such as canoeing, walking, pony trekking, cycling, river fishing and much more.

The generally slow moving, broad waters of the River Wye are ideal for canoeing. Canoes or Kayaks can be hired at Glasbury, a few miles upstream or in Hay itself. It's a novel way to view the amazingly beautiful countryside and with luck you may catch a glimpse of a kingfisher or heron as you paddle gently downstream; the activity is suitable for beginners or the more experienced.

Walkers of all abilities are well catered for, whether it be a gentle stroll along the river bank or a vigorous hike through the Black Mountains. Hay Bluff and the curiously named Lord Hereford's Knob are two peaks easily climbed from Hay; both give fantastic views over the Brecon Beacons, Radnorshire and Herefordshire.

A narrow winding road climbs steeply out of town up the mountain, crosses the Gospel Pass then drops down into the rugged remote valley of the Vale of Ewyas at Capel-y-ffin from where some excellent high level walks are possible.

Cyclists with strong limbs may also be tempted to try the challenging but exciting route over the Gospel Pass to Llanthony. A more

leisurely destination would be the Golden Valley in Herefordshire, with its lush farmland and picturesque villages.

Another leisure pursuit well established in this area is pony trekking. Bridleways abound and the steep sided valleys, open moorland and flat topped ridges make it one of the most popular riding areas in Wales. The experienced rider and novices alike are catered for with half or full day treks offered.

Attractions Nearby

Brobury House Gardens (12m/ 9.5km)
Brobury
HR3 6BS
☎ 01981 500229
www.broburyhouse.co.uk
Restored terraced Victorian garden on the banks of the river Wye.

Dore Abbey (16m/26km)
Abbey Dore HR2 0AA
www.doreabbey.co.uk

Above: Dore Abbey

In the 1630s the ruins of the old Cistercian abbey in the beautiful Golden Valley were partially rebuilt to form a parish church. Threatened by closure in 1993 it was rescued by a vigorous local campaign and now visitors may still enjoy the atmosphere of ancient tranquillity and colourful stained glass windows.

Capel-y-ffin (9m/14km)

Follow the narrow byway on its serpentine route over Gospel Pass to the secluded Vale of Ewyas. Visit the tiny St Mary's Church, one of the smallest in the country, with its strange lopsided belfry. Savour the tranquillity of the place before going for a walk or travelling further down the valley to Llanthony Priory.

Hotels and Dining

Try the local Tourist Information Centre, see Essential Contacts for details.

Kilverts Hotel

The Bull Ring
HR3 5AG
☎ 01497 821042
www.kilverts.co.uk
Town centre hotel with attractive secluded garden and a reputation for good beer.

The Old Black Lion

Lion Street
HR3 5AD
☎ 01497 820841
www.oldblacklion.co.uk
Historic old inn, exposed timber beams and lots of character.

Baskerville Arms Hotel (1.5m/2.5km)

Clyro
HR3 5RZ
☎ 01497 820670
www.baskervillearms.co.uk
Traditional country inn with cosy rooms and log fires.

Aberllynfi B+B (6m/9.5km)

Aberllynfi House, Glasbury
HR3 5NT
☎ 01497 847107
Listed Georgian house in idyllic location on the banks of the river Wye with walled garden, tennis court and private jetty.

Black Mountain Lodge (3m/5km)

Glasbury
HR3 5PT
☎ 01497 847897
www.blackmountainlodge.co.uk
Converted 19th century stables are home to this guest house in a rural location in the Wye valley.

The Swan at Hay

Church Street
HR3 5DQ
☎ 01497 821188
www.swanathay.co.uk
Award winning restaurant in elegant Georgian coaching inn.

The Three Tuns

Broad Street
HR3 5DB
☎ 01497 821855
www.three-tuns.com
Carefully restored after a fire in 2005 the oldest pub in town offers a choice of dining area; restaurant, bar or paved, heated patio.

Landmark Trust

Maesyronen Chapel
Small cottage adjacent to ancient chapel, sleeps up to 4.

Events

Hay Festival

The annual festival of literature and the arts has been running for over 20 years. It features writers, comedians, musicians and politicians in a packed programme of events held in the town in early summer. You will need to book accommodation early if you want to attend.

Essential Contacts

Hay-on-Wye Tourist Information Office

Oxford Road
HR3 5DG
☎ 01497 820144

Wye Valley Canoes (4m/6.5km)

The Boat House, Glasbury-on-Wye
HR3 5NP
☎ 01497 847213
www.wyevalleycanoes.co.uk
Paddle downstream to Hay or Whitney. Return by minibus.

Paddles and Peddles

15 Castle Street
HR3 5DF
☎ 01497 820604
www.canoehire.co.uk
Canoe or kayak hire from Hay with return transport.

Drover Holidays

3 Oxford Road
HR3 5AJ
☎ 01497 821134
www.droverholidays.co.uk
Cycle hire.

Tregoyd Mountain Riders (4.5m/7.5km)

Tregoyd, Three Cocks
LD3 0SP
☎ 01497 847351
www.tregoydriding.co.uk
Pony Trekking.

The Grange Trekking Centre (7m/11km)

Capel-y-ffin
NP7 7NP
☎ 01873 890215
www.grangetrekking.co.uk
Pony trekking.

Black Mountain Activities (7m/11km)

Three Cocks
LD3 0SD
☎ 01497 847897
www.blackmountain.co.uk
Gorge walking, high level ropes, rock climbing and other activities.

Knighton and Presteigne, Powys

Getting There

By Road
Knighton is on the A4113 from Ludlow.

By Rail
The Heart of Wales line from Swansea to Shrewsbury passes through Knighton.

By Coach
There are national coaches to Newtown, Shrewsbury or Hereford and then onward by local bus.

Above: Knighton

Left: Presteigne

Background Briefing

Knighton and Presteigne are on the Welsh border with England in an area known as the Welsh Marches. The name comes from the Marcher Lords who ruled these parts and often bore the title Earl of March. Although not as well known as the National Parks in Wales the wooded Marches countryside is never the less stunningly beautiful with mountains and moorlands, farms, wooded river valleys and many small villages with half-timbered buildings and castles. It is an area rich in history as the ancient forts, castles and other historic sites illustrate.

Knighton or Tref-y-Clawdd in Welsh, which means "Town on the Dyke", is the only town that is situated on Offa's Dyke. The Offa's Dyke Centre in the town has exhibitions about the dyke and information about the Offa's Dyke National Trail, a 177m/283km long distance walk which runs from Prestatyn in the north to Chepstow in the south. Knighton is also the start of another National Trail, Glyndwr's Way, a 135m/216km walk through mid Wales finishing at Welshpool. The 86m/138km regional cycle route, the Radnor Ring, which passes through both Knighton and Presteigne, is a delightful scenic ride. The town has some steeply climbing streets known as The Narrows, with half timbered buildings dating from the 17th century. Today The Narrows are the place to shop for antiques, crafts and souvenirs or enjoy a quiet drink.

Presteigne or Llanandras in Welsh is a medieval market town with buildings dating back to the 14th century and was once the county town of Radnorshire. There is a town trail leaflet which

Above: Offa's Dyke

will guide you round the many historic buildings in this small, quiet and unspoilt town. The Judges Lodging which now houses an award winning museum is not to be missed and the outstanding medieval parish church displays the recently restored Prestigne Tapestry on its north wall. The Flemish tapestry created about 1510 shows Christ's entry into Jerusalem. In early May the church houses an art show featuring works by painters, silversmiths and sculptors. The Mid Border Arts organisation also promotes a wide range of arts activities throughout the year at the Assembly Rooms.

Places to visit

The Spaceguard Centre
Llanshay Lane, Knighton
LD7 1LW
☎ 01547 520247
www.spaceguarduk.com
An independent astronomical observatory which monitors objects such as asteroids or comets for the likelihood of collisions with earth. It has several powerful telescopes and a range of other equipment - including a satellite weather station, a planetarium, a seismometer and a camera obscura. It is open for tours Wednesday to Sunday.

The Judge's Lodging
Broad Street, Presteigne
LD8 2AD
☎ 01544 260650
www.judgeslodging.org.uk
A hands on Victorian museum it was originally opened in 1829 as a combination of court room, accommodation for judges, and administrative centre for the county of Radnorshire. You can explore the courtroom and cells, plus the many rooms of a grand Victorian residence.

Attractions Nearby

Stokesay Castle (English Heritage) (19m/30km)
Craven Arms, Shropshire
SY7 9AH
☎ 01588 672 544

www.english-heritage.org.uk/stokesaycastle
Just over the border is Stokesay Castle, the finest and best preserved 13th century fortified manor house in England. It is virtually unaltered since 1291. It also has a fine timber framed Jacobean gatehouse.

Hotels and Dining

Try the local Tourist Information Centre, see Essential Contacts for details.

Milebrook House Hotel
Milebrook, Knighton
LD7 1LT
☎ 01547 528 632
www.milebrookhouse.co.uk
The AA 3 star, 2 rosette, hotel is surrounded by 3 acres of gardens including a kitchen garden which supplies many of the vegetables served in the restaurant. There is fly fishing available on the River Teme adjoining the hotel.

The Old Vicarage
Norton, Presteigne
LD8 2EN
☎ 01544 260038
www.oldvicarage-nortonrads.co.uk
This award winning 5 star guest accommodation with the coveted Wales Gold Award has been restored to retain its period charm and authenticity. Surrounded by an attractive garden in the heart of the Welsh Marches it is a splendid rural retreat.

Radnorshire Arms Hotel
High Street, Presteigne
LD8 2BE
☎ 01544 267406
www.radnorshirearmshotel.com
The Radnorshire Arms is a warm and welcoming family run hotel nestled amidst rolling hills and wonderful open countryside. This Grade 2 Jacobean listed building, with its original exposed beams and

timber panelled walls, has an atmosphere of comfort and elegance.

The Stagg Inn Ltd
Titley, Kington, Herefordshire
HR5 3RL
☎ 01544 230221
www.thestagg.co.uk
The Stagg was the first pub to be awarded the coveted Michelin Star for its food and it regularly appears in the Good Pub Guide.

Landmark Trust
Stockwell Farm, Old Radnor
Dates back to c.1600, sleeps up to 6.

Events

Presteigne Festival of Music and the Arts
www.presteignefestival.com

Sheep Music – contemporary music
www.sheepmusic.info

Llanberis, Gwynedd

Getting There

By Road

From the north take M56 then the A55 to junction11. From the midlands take the A5 from the M54 and from the south use the scenic A470.

By Rail

The nearest railway station is Bangor; there are frequent local buses from Bangor.

By Coach

National coaches run to Bangor and then onward by local bus.

Above: Llanberis Pass

Background Briefing

Llanberis, in the heart of Snowdonia National Park, is a honey pot location for walkers, climbers and other visitors. The star attraction is of course Snowdon (Yr Wyddfa in Welsh) at 3,560ft/1085m the highest mountain in England and Wales. The route to the top from Llanberis follows the railway track and is the longest but least demanding of the many ways up the mountain, or you can of course, take the train to the top. Almost as famous as Snowdon is Pete's Eats, the legendary cafe in the centre of town; it is the place to eat before and after a day in the mountains.

Llanberis owes its existence to the slate in the surrounding hills, evidence of the extensive quarrying in the now redundant quarries being clearly visible across the lake from the town. The legacy of the slate industry now provides the visitor with many attractions in the town such as the National Slate Museum and the Llyn Padarn narrow gauge railway which follows part of the route of the quarry railway; you can also visit the old Dinorwig Quarry Hospital. Perched on a small rocky

Above: Dolbadarn Castle

outcrop some 80ft/24m above Llyn Padarn is Dolbadarn Castle, built by Llewelyn the Great in the 13th century. The round keep is the only remaining structure but surprisingly there is an almost hidden narrow staircase, leading to a small viewing platform at the top of the tower.

Padarn Country Park, as well as containing the museum and railway, has many waymarked walks so if you want something gentler than the mountains this is the place to go.

Nearby are Caernarfon, with its splendid castle, and Bangor, a university town with a Victorian pier which gives the impression that you could walk to Anglesey, which

you cannot. If you want to visit Anglesey you will need to use one of the two historic bridges, Thomas Telford's suspension bridge built in 1826 or the Britannia Railway Bridge originally built by Robert Stevenson in 1850 and rebuilt after a fire in 1970 with a road on top of the box girders carrying the railway line.

Places to visit

Snowdon Mountain Railway

Llanberis
☎ 0870 458 0033
www.snowdonrailway.co.uk
The rack and pinion railway provides a truly spectacular journey from Llanberis to the top of Snowdon. The dramatic landscape and scenery on a fine day is something not to be missed, however the weather in the mountains cannot be guaranteed, but the journey is always interesting even if there is low cloud. There is the new sympathetically designed Snowdon Summit Visitor Centre, Hafod Eryri at the top, featuring a curved granite roof and panoramic windows, manufactured in non-reflective glass, to give visitors

Above: The Lake Railway

unimpaired views across the mighty Snowdonia range.

Visitors would be well advised to book in advance or as soon as they get to Llanberis as there can be long queues at busy times.

Padarn Country Park

Quarry Hospital
Padarn Country Park
Llanberis
☎ 01286 870892
www.llanberis.org/padarn.htm
The Padarn Country Park has two Sites of Special Scientific Interest, the Coed Allt Wen woodlands and the lake, Llyn Padarn. It has many waymarked walks including nature, woodland and industrial trails and a 5m/8km walk around the lake. The Old Dinorwig Quarry Hospital is now a museum; it has free displays and information including some of the original equipment from the 1800s, such as a restored ward and operating theatre, plus an original X-Ray Machine and other medical equipment. There are also displays about the park. The Padarn Watersports Centre offers visitors canoeing, windsurfing, fun-boats and sailing at reasonable prices. The old Vivian Slate Quarry within the country park is now a diving school catering for all from beginners to experienced divers.

National Slate Museum

Padarn Country Park,
☎ 01286 870630
www.museumwales.ac.uk/en/slate
The Slate Museum is another of the National Museum of Wales' excellent sites. Situated in the old Victorian workshops it looks as if the quarrymen have only just left. There is a site tour including the workshops, iron and brass foundry, forges, loco shed and the water powered machinery that made the tools for quarrying slate, not forgetting the largest working watermill in mainland Britain. There are demonstrations of slate splitting by craftsmen and you can also see the living conditions of the quarrymen at different times in a row of quarrymen's houses.

Llanberis Lake Railway

Padarn Country Park
☎ 01286 870549
www.lake-railway.co.uk
A scenic 5m/8km round trip on the delightful narrow gauge steam train which runs along the shores of Lake Padarn to Penllyn, gives stunning views of Snowdon and will take about an hour. Part of the route

Above: Padarn Country Park

Above: National Slate Museum

the trains, hauled by vintage steam engines, follow is the old 1845 slate railway route.

Ropes & Ladders

Gilfach Ddu
Padarn Country Park
LL55 4TY
☎ 01286 872310
www.ropesandladders.co.uk
Padarn Country Park with its wonderful views of the lake and mountains is the setting for the exciting aerial challenge of this high ropes course, with climbing, leaps, a giant swing and zip lines. An instructor will provide you with all your safety equipment and be on hand to encourage and advise.

Electric Mountain

Llanberis
☎ 01286 870636
www.fhc.co.uk/electric_mountain.htm
Under Elidir Mountain Dinorwig hydro-electric power station is situated in the largest man-made cavern in Europe. Water from a lake on top of the mountain is released at times of high demand for electricity and as it falls, it turns turbines inside the mountain to generate instant power. When there is a low demand for electricity, the water is pumped back to the higher lake, ready to be used again.

The visitor centre explains the technology used at this underground hydro-electric power station and visitors can also take a guided tour.

Attractions Nearby

Caernarfon Castle (Cadw) (7m/11km)

Caernarfon with its magnificent castle is just 7m/11km away. With its massive walls and battlements it is probably the most impressive of all of all the castles built by Edward I. It was the scene in1969 of the investiture of the Prince of Wales. The castle also houses the Regimental Museum of the Royal Welch Fusiliers, Wales's oldest regiment.

Hotels and Dining

Try the local Tourist Information Centre, see Essential Contacts for details.

Seiont Manor Hotel

Llanrug, Caernafon
LL55 2AQ
☎ 0845 072 7550
www.handpickedhotels.co.uk/hotels/seiont-manor
Situated in 150 acres of grounds this 3 star hotel advertises a 40 foot indoor swimming pool, a health club with sauna, health and beauty treatment room and fitness gym. It also has 2 Rosette restaurants and a newly opened conservatory brasserie.

Dol Peris Hotel

High Street, Llanberis
LL55 4HA
☎ 01286 870350
www.dolperis.com
In the centre of Llanberis the hotel set in its own grounds is a grade 2 listed building built in the 1850s.

Gwesty Plas Coch

High Street , Llanberis
LL55 4HB
☎ 01286 872122
www.plas-coch.co.uk
A 4 star B&B, prices include a packed lunch for all guests.

The Legacy Royal Victoria Hotel

Llanberis
LL55 4TY
☎ 0870 8329903
In 30 acres of garden and woodland this hotel occupies a prime position between the two lakes Padarn and Peris.

Peak Restaurant

86 High Street , Llanberis
LL55 4SU
☎ 01286 872777
www.peakrestaurant.co.uk
Chef Angela Dwyer has had rave reviews for her cooking skills over the years and worked as head chef in top London restaurants before coming to Llanberis.

Sopna Tandoori Restaurant

Felin Wen, Rhosbodrual
Caernarfon
LL55 2BB
☎ 01286 675222
In 2007 Sopna Tandoori won the Wales national Curry House of the year award. It is about 3miles north of Llanberis.

Pete's Eats

40 High Street, Llanberis
LL55 4EU
☎ 01286 870117
www.petes-eats.co.uk
A pint of tea and one of Pete's hearty meals, the end of a perfect day on the mountains.

Events

Snowdon Race

July

Snowdon Marathon

October

Essential Contacts

Tourist Information Centre

41A High Street, Llanberis
LL55 4EU
☎ 01286 870765

Llanberis Lake Cruises

☎ 07974 716418

Vivian Diving Centre

Parc Gwledig Padarn
LL55 4TY
☎ 01286 870889
www.divevivian.com

Llandeilo, Carmarthenshire

Getting There

By Road

Llandeilo lies at the crossroads of the A40 and the A483 between Brecon and Carmarthen.

By Rail

Llandeilo station is on the Heart of Wales, Swansea to Shrewsbury line.

By Coach

There are coaches to Carmarthen then local bus to Llandeilo.

Above: National Botanic Garden of Wales

Background Briefing

Llandeilo is the jewel in the Tywi Valley. It has everything one could wish for in a small country town: a long history starting in Roman times, a scenic location surrounded by farms, woodland, hills and valleys, adjacent to the Brecon Beacons National Park. It also has attractive coloured houses and winding streets full of chic shops, galleries and boutiques. Much of the town is a conservation area with many Georgian buildings; the Llandeilo Town Heritage Trail gives lots of information about the town's buildings and is a pleasant way to familiarise yourself with the town. It is a veritable shopper's paradise with shops selling a wide range of goods from exclusive ladies fashions, jewellers, antiques and art galleries to florists and kitchenware.

Nearby is Dinefwr Castle and Park with trees thought to be up to 700 years old in the Castle Woods nature reserve, whilst 4 miles away to the south east, perched on its crag, is the romantic ruin of Carreg Cennen Castle.

Also nearby are the magnificent gardens of Aberglasney and of course the National Botanic Garden of Wales, both having collections of rare plants and much of interest for all garden lovers.

As well as being an attractive historical town with much to offer, Llandeilo is an excellent base for exploring the wider area of south west Wales. A trip west to Carmarthen should include a visit to the Carmarthenshire Museum at Abergwili, with displays from the earliest times up to World War II. Brecon Beacons National Park is adjacent to the eastern edge of the town and the Gower with its wonderful beaches is only a half hour drive away.

Places to visit

Dinefwr Castle (Cadw), Park and Newton House (NT)

Llandeilo
SA19 6RT
☎ 01558 824512
www.castlewales.com/dinefwr.html

One mile to the west of the town are the ruins of the 12th century Dinefwr Castle, an excellent view point of the Tywi Valley. In the landscaped Dinefwr Park (NT), which has herds of fallow deer and White Park cattle, you will find Newton House a country house with some 1912-style rooms, exhibition rooms, tea-room and

Above left: The old town, Llandeilo; **left:** Newton House, Dinefwr Park; **Above:** Aberglasney Hall and Gardens

National Trust shop. There are also scenic walks and Castle Woods Nature Reserve to explore.

Attractions Nearby

National Botanic Garden of Wales (10m/16km)

Llanarthne, Carmarthenshire
SA32 8HG
☎ 01558 668768
www.gardenofwales.org.uk
A must see for all gardeners and plant lovers, set in a 200 year old park, it combines the historical with the modern having the world's largest single span glasshouse designed by Norman Foster and Partners and a collection of over 100,000 plants, some rare and endangered. It has the longest herbaceous border in Europe, water features, a double walled garden, a tropical house and much more.

Aberglasney Hall and Gardens (4m/6km)

Llangathen, Carmarthenshire
SA32 8QH
☎ 01558 668998
www.aberglasney.org
Set in the Twyi valley the site has a long history dating back to 15th century. The property is now owned by the Aberglasney Restoration Trust who are working to restore both the garden, advertised as one of the finest in Wales, and the hall to their former glory. The gardens are extensive with many rare plants and something of interest all year round.

Carreg Cennen Castle (4.5m/7km)

Trapp, Llandeilo
SA19 6UA
☎ 01558 822291
www.carregcennencastle.com
In the North West corner of the Brecon Beacons National Park the ruins of the Welsh Carreg Cennen Castle managed by Cadw sits on a crag high above the River Cennen.

The steep ascent is well worth the effort as you will be rewarded with spectacular views of the surrounding countryside as well as an ancient and romantic ruin to explore.

Carmarthenshire County Museum (12m/20km)

Abergwili, Carmarthen
SA31 2JG
☎ 01267 228696
The museum is housed in the old St. Davids bishop's palace, a building in use since 1290. There are displays of local archaeology, pottery, portraits, landscape paintings, Welsh furniture, costume, a Victorian schoolroom and life on the farm.

Hotels and Dining

Try the local Tourist Information Centre, see Essential Contacts for details.

Something Special

The Cawdor

Rhosmaen Street, Llandeilo
SA19 6EN
☎ 0800 988 3002
www.thecawdor.com
A mix of old and new this 4 star boutique hotel is housed in a Georgian Building in the centre of town. The hotel has an eclectic mix of period features and contemporary design. The restaurant serves both traditional and modern dishes using locally sourced ingredients.

Landmark Trust

Pacton's Tower Lodge,
Llanarthney
Near National Botanic Gardens
Small cottage, great view, sleeps up to 5.

Fronlas

7 Thomas Street, Llandeilo
SA19 6LB
☎ 01558 824733
www. fronlas.com

An eco friendly, 5 star, boutique style B&B offering an organic breakfast, in the centre of Llandeilo.

The Plough Inn

Rhosmaen, Llandeilo
SA19 6NP
☎ 01558 823 431
www. ploughrhosmaen.com
An AA 3 star hotel and restaurant with gym and sauna.

The Fig Tree Restaurant and Wine Bar

Dryslwyn Fawr, Llanarthne
SA32 8JQ
☎ 01558 668 187
www.thefigtreerestaurant.co.uk
This restaurant in the Twyi valley with views of Dryslwyn Castle and Paxton's Tower has a modern menu and extensive wine list. 4 & 5 star holiday cottages are also available at Dryslwyn Fawr.

Events

Flower and Music festival

Early summer.

Monthly Antiques Fair

1st Saturday of each month.

Country Market

Weekly on Fridays.

Llandudno, Conwy C.B.

Getting There

By Road

The A470 to Llandudno leaves the A55 at J19. Alternatively, take the B5115 from J20.

By Rail

There is a regular train service to Llandudno station but on some services it may be necessary to change at Llandudno Junction.

By Coach

Coach services call at Mostyn Broadway coach park.

Top: Punch & Judy; Middle: St George's Hotel on the promenade; Bottom: The pier

Background Briefing

The ever popular seaside resort of Llandudno is one of the few in Wales that benefits from the twofold attraction of full resort facilities combined with great scenic beauty. The dominating feature of the landscape is the limestone hills, in particular the Great and Little Ormes. There are two beaches: the North Shore is nearest the town centre and has a pier, bandstand, children's paddling pool and Punch and Judy show; the quieter West Shore has a model boating pool, putting green and sand dunes. The broad Promenade on the North Shore follows the gentle curve of the bay from the limestone cliffs of the Great Orme through to its counterparts on the Little Orme; flanking the Promenade are handsome three and four storey Victorian terraces. Much of the town of Llandudno that we see today was built as a result of a decision in 1849 by Lord Mostyn, owner of most of the land around, to build a 'model resort' on what were then fields on the flat land below the Great Orme. The layout of the town was carefully planned with broad streets and a restriction on the height of buildings which has not been breached today.

The pier, at 2295ft / 700m, is the longest in Wales; opened in 1878 it is still a magnet for visitors, with its kiosks, cafe, bar, amusements and fishing area, not to mention the superb views over the bay and the town. Nearby the Marine Drive offers a scenic route around the Great Orme headland. The Happy Valley Gardens are a careful blend of nature and horticulture and lie on a steeply sloping site above the pier; in a sheltered position they are a good place to sit and relax amid the trees and flowers. Those not of a nervous disposition can take the cable car from here to the Great Orme summit in the summer months. At the top of the gardens the ski slope provides entertainment for participants and spectators alike. A path leads from here to the Great Orme summit (679ft/ 207m), passing the old copper mine and the tramway on the way.

The West Shore can be reached by following the broad boulevard of Gloddaeth Street, along which the road train runs in summer. Alternatively climb up to Haulfre Gardens, an attractive place with flowerbeds and mature trees leading to a footpath that contours around the base of Great Orme, giving wonderful views of the Conwy estuary with the dark brooding mountains of Snowdonia behind. The West Shore beach is sand backed by shingle and at low tide seems to stretch as far as the eye can see; beyond the beach cafe sand dunes line the beach leading towards Deganwy.

In addition to the usual seaside attractions the arts are well catered for: there is a major theatre complex at Venue Cymru, a museum and two small art galleries. The town's major art gallery, Oriel Mostyn, is scheduled to reopen in 2010 following a major expansion project.

Close by to Llandudno are the historic walled town of Conwy, the beautiful Conwy Valley and the attractions of Snowdonia.

Places to visit

Great Orme Tramway
Victoria Station
Church Walks
LL30 2NB
☎ 01492 879306
www.greatormetramway.co.uk
Now over a century old the cable hauled tram continues to delight young and old with its ride to the summit of Great Orme.

Llandudno Ski and Snowboard Centre

Great Orme
LL30 2QL
☎ 01492 874707
www.llandudnoskislope.co.uk
Learn to ski or practice your skills on the dry sky slope on the flanks of the Great Orme. Alternatively try the toboggan run, an exciting ride 750 metres long with tight bends.

Great Orme Mines

Great Orme
LL30 2XG
☎ 01492 870447
www.greatormemines.info
Walk through tunnels hacked out by Bronze Age miners on a self guided underground tour of the 4000 year old copper mine workings.

Great Orme Country Park

Visible from all over town the massive limestone headland is a great attraction. The tram, the cable car and the road all converge on the summit but there is a multitude of paths up to and over this country park and nature reserve. Wild flowers such as thrift, sea campion, rock rose and thyme abound. And don't be surprised if you come face to face with a herd of goats; these Kashmir goats were introduced in Victorian times and seem to thrive on the headland.

Attractions Nearby

Welsh Mountain Zoo (8m/12.5km)

Colwyn Bay
LL28 5UY
☎ 01492 532 938
www.welshmountainzoo.org
Well established zoological garden overlooking Colwyn Bay.

Colwyn Bay Beach (4.5m/7.5km)

Stretching for three miles from picturesque Rhos Harbour to Penmaenhead, the beach is broad and sandy, with a good selection of eateries at Rhos.

Hotels and Dining

Try the local Tourist Information Centre, see Essential Contacts for details.

Something Special

St Georges Hotel The Promenade

LL30 2LG
☎ 01492 877544
www.stgeorgeswales.co.uk
This historic hotel has a prime site on the Promenade with sea views from some rooms. Refurbished to the highest standards it presents modern decor and facilities in a magnificent Victorian building.

Bodysgallen Hall Hotel Restaurant and Spa (2.5m/4.5km)

Llandudno
LL30 1RS
☎ 01492 584466
www.bodysgallen.com
Step back in time at this old manor house now owned by the National Trust and operating as a luxury country house hotel. A grade I listed building, mainly 17th century but with a 13th century tower, the hotel is set in 200 acres of parkland and has attractive formal gardens. The health and fitness spa offers all the latest treatments and a 50 foot swimming pool.

The Lighthouse B+B (2.5m/4.0km)

Marine Drive, Great Orme's Head
LL30 2XD
☎ 01492 876819
www.lighthouse-llandudno.co.uk
A unique B+B in the former lighthouse, the views are superb and the building retains many original features.

Escape Boutique B&B

48 Church Walks
LL30 2HL
☎ 01492 877776
www.escapebandb.co.uk
A five star B+B with contemporary styling and convenient location.

The Seahorse Restaurant 7 Church Walks

LL30 2HD
☎ 01492 875 315
A relaxed atmosphere with an emphasis on fish dishes.

Carlo's Restaurant

2 Pleasant Street, Llandudno
☎ 01492 875722
Popular Italian restaurant.

Events

Llandudno Transport Festival

May

Llandudno Victorian Extravaganza

May

North Wales Cricket Festival

August

Celtic Winter Fayre

November

Essential Contacts

Tourist Information Centre

Library Building, Mostyn Street
LL30 2RP
☎ 01492 577577

Venue Cymru

The Promenade
LL30 1BB
☎ 01492 872000
www.venuecymru.co.uk
A full range of performing arts in a modern 1500 seat theatre.

Llangollen, Denbighshire

Getting There

By Road
On the A5 between Oswestry and Corwen.

By Rail
By train to Ruabon on the Shrewsbury to Chester line then onward by local bus.

By Coach
Limited service to Llangollen; more frequent service to Chester from where local buses can be taken to Llangollen.

Top and above right: Llangollen; **Above left:** Corwen Hilfort

Background Briefing

The bustling tourist town of Llangollen sits astride the River Dee a few miles from the English border. Here the pure waters of the river fight their way over and between massive slabs of rock before plunging beneath the stone arches of the old bridge. All around the high hills look down on the small town. Nature has been kind to Llangollen and so has man. The river and the hills are complemented by man's works: the riverside railway station introduces a sense of nostalgia for a bygone age; the canal and its horse-drawn boats blend quietly into the countryside; the ruined castle on its hill imbues the scene with romantic mystery.

The most popular attraction in town is probably the railway. Many are attracted by the fascination of steam engines and while there are several restored railways in Wales this is a rare example of a standard gauge line. It runs for over seven miles through the beautiful ever changing scenery of the Dee valley and provides an unforgettable experience.

Just up the hill from the station is Llangollen Wharf. From here a regular service of horse drawn passenger narrow boats operates between Easter and October offering a 45 minute round trip on the tranquil waters of the Llangollen Canal. Also available from the Wharf are motor boat trips to, and across, the famous Pontcysyllte Aqueduct.

There are several historic houses to visit in the area. In Llangollen itself is Plas Newydd, once home to the famous 'Ladies of Llangollen'. A short distance away, Chirk Castle is an imposing stately home dating back to medieval times while Erddig is a magnificent country house where the life of the servants is depicted in equal measure to the life of their masters.

The Dee valley is a great place to explore on foot. The Llangollen History Trail is a 6m/9km route which links many of the area's historical features: the canal towpath to the Horseshoe Falls, a weir constructed on the river to divert water into the canal; Llantysilio Church with its relics from medieval times; the ruins of the once powerful Valle Crucis Abbey; Eliseg's Pillar, the remains of an 8th century cross; Dinas Bran Castle, the ruined fortress of Welsh ruler Gruffud ap Madoc. Offa's Dyke National Trail passes near the town and travelling northwards passes beneath the spectacular limestone cliffs of Eglwyseg on the way to the curiously named World's End.

If you fancy getting away from the tourist trail you could visit the nearby small town of Corwen. It does have two tourist attractions, Rug Chapel and Llangar Church but by and large most people pass it by. It's an unassuming place with a few small shops and cafes but much quieter than Llangollen and with a strong Welsh character; you'll hear the Welsh language spoken often here and there is a striking statue to local hero Owain Glyndwr. There are some pleasant riverside walks and there's a prominent hill fort just out of town.

Places to visit

Plas Newydd
Hill Street
LL20 8AW
☎ 01978 861314
Fascinating old black and white timbered house on the edge of town. Much of what you can see today was the result of work by the celebrated 'Ladies of Llangollen'. These two young women from Ireland set up home together in the then much smaller house in 1780. Over a period of 50 years they extended the house and introduced many ornate wood carvings derived from diverse sources. They achieved celebrity status and were visited by the great and the good of the time, some of them apparently bringing with them additions for the house.

Llangollen Railway
The Station, Abbey Road
LL20 8SN
☎ 01978 860979
www.llangollen-railway.co.uk
Take a steam hauled train from the riverside station for a 7½m/12km trip along the beautiful unspoilt Dee Valley to the pleasant riverside village of Carrog. From small beginnings in 1975 this restoration of a standard gauge line goes from strength to strength with regular extensions to the length of line and now attracting over 100,000 passengers a year.

Llangollen Wharf
Wharf Hill
☎ 01978 860702
www.horsedrawnboats.co.uk
Leisurely horse drawn cruises or longer motorised trips to the Pontcysyllte aqueduct.

Llangollen Local History Museum
Parade Street
☎ 01978 862862
www.llangollenmuseum.org.uk
Housed in a modern building in the centre of town this small volunteer run museum explains the history of the town through displays and photographs; it packs a lot of information into a small space and is free of charge.

Castell Dinas Bran
Ruinous archways and gnarled fingers of stone pointing skywards are all that remain of this castle perched on a hill overlooking the town. But the air of mystery and the wonderful views make it worth the effort of the steep climb to get there.

Above: Pontcysyllte Aqueduct; **Above right:** Narrow boats moored at Llangollen

Left: Chirk Castle; Right: Valle Crucis Abbey

Valle Crucis Abbey

LL20 8DD

☎ 01978 860326

Much survives of this once important abbey, established by Cistercian monks in the 13th century in a secluded valley. Look out for the vaulted chapter house, the finely carved rose window on the west front and the original monks' fish pond. The name Valle Crucis means in Latin valley of the cross. The cross in question was built by Eliseg around four hundred years before the abbey and can still be visited nearby, but only the column now survives.

Attractions Nearby

Pontcysyllte Aqueduct (World Heritage Site) (4.5m/7km)

Thomas Telford's great engineering masterpiece carries the canal across the Dee valley on a series of massive arches. Alongside the canal trough runs the narrow towpath, an airy, scary promenade with only iron railings to protect the walker from the vertical drop, 126ft/38m at its highest point.

Erddig House (NT) (13.5m/21.5km)

Wrexham

LL13 0YT

☎ 01978 315151

A large country house set in extensive parkland with a restored formal garden. In addition to the state rooms, the servants' kitchen and other work rooms are well preserved.

Chirk Castle (NT) (7m/11km)

Chirk

LL14 5AF

☎ 01691 777701

This massive Marcher fortress dates back to the time of Edward I. Unusually it has remained in use, initially as a military structure and then as a stately home, ever since. It stands in parkland on the hillside overlooking Chirk and has fine gardens with terraces, rock gardens and clipped yew hedges.

Rug Chapel (Cadw) (11.5m/18.5km)

Rug, Corwen

LL21 9BT

☎ 01490 412025

A small chapel built for private use

in the 17th century, it has a richly decorated interior. The contrasting simply furnished medieval Llangar church nearby can be visited by arrangement with the custodian at Rug. While at Rug why not visit the organic farm shop; you could even try one of their home-produced bison burgers!

Hotels and Dining

Try the local Tourist Information Centre, see Essential Contacts for details.

Something Special

Landmark Trust

Plas Uchaf, nr Corwen

Hall house, c. 1400, sleeps up to 4.

Gales Hotel and Winebar

18 Bridge Street

LL20 8PF

☎ 01978 860089

www.galesofllangollen.co.uk

Spread across two buildings, a former Georgian townhouse and a much older timber framed building, the hotel boasts individually designed rooms, some retaining original features such as exposed beams and wattle and daub walls.

White Waters Country Hotel

Berwyn Road
LL20 8BS
☎ 01978 861661
www.whitewatershotel.co.uk
Superb location overlooking the River Dee and Dinas Bran Castle, with log fires in winter and patio dining in summer.

Wild Pheasant Hotel

Berwyn Road
LL20 8AD
☎ 01978 860629
www.wildpheasanthotel.co.uk
Old meets new at this hotel just outside the town centre. A striking modern extension has been added to the original 19th century building and the hotel is set in beautiful gardens with stunning views of the surrounding countryside.

Chainbridge Hotel (2m/3km)

Berwyn
LL20 8BS
☎ 01978 860215
www.chainbridgehotel.com
In a splendid rural location between the placid canal and the rushing River Dee; watch the steam trains go by too.

Bryn Howel Hotel (2.5m/4.5km)

Trevor
LL20 7UW
☎ 01978 860331
www.brynhowel.com
Popular family owned hotel and restaurant in a magnificent country house.

Britannia Inn (4 m/7km)

Horseshoe Pass
LL20 8DW
☎ 01978 860144
www.britinn.com
Comfortable accommodation in historic inn at the foot of the Horseshoe Pass.

The Cornmill

Dee Lane
LL20 8PN
☎ 01978 869555
www.cornmill-llangollen.co.uk
Centuries old corn mill in the centre of town converted to a pub/restaurant in 2000. Exposed beams and mill machinery with a decking area overhanging the river.

Caesar's Restaurant

Dee Lane
LL20 8PN
☎ 01978 860133
Intimate riverside restaurant in town centre.

Events

International Eisteddfod

The world famous Eisteddfod has taken place in Llangollen every year since 1947. Although based in the purpose built Royal Pavilion and Festival Field just outside town the singing and dancing spills out into the streets of the town with performers from around the world in their colourful costumes. Be aware that this is a very popular event and accommodation books up very early.
www.international-eisteddfod.co.uk

Llangollen Fringe Festival

A summer festival of comedy and music; follows the Eisteddfod
www.llangollenfringe.co.uk

Hot Air Balloon Festival

All manner of weird and wonderful balloons take to the skies above Llangollen on a weekend in September.
www.hotairballoonfestival.co.uk

The Gardening Show

Summer show of all things horticultural at the Royal International Pavilion.
www.thegardeningshow.co.uk

Food Festival

An autumn food fest held at the Royal Pavilion.
www.llangollenfoodfestival.co.uk

Left: Llangollen Canal

Getting There

By Road

Llanidloes lies just off the A470.

Rail

The nearest rail station is at Caersws (6 miles), onward by local bus.

Coach

Coaches from Birmingham stop at Llanidloes.

Background Briefing

At the very heart of Wales, nestling beneath the great bulk of Plynlimon, highest point in mid-Wales, lies the historic small town of Llanidloes. Once a hive of industry it now offers a haven to visitors seeking a refuge for a few days from the stresses and strains of modern urban life; a chance to relish the slower pace of life, the clean mountain air, the clear rushing streams, the tranquillity of a forest glade.

Llanidloes has the distinction of being the first town encountered by the infant River Severn on its long journey from the source on Plynlimon to its outfall into the Bristol Channel, 220m/352km in total. It has a long history, going back as far as the 7th century when St Idloes established a church by the river. The Normans arrived as early as 1066 and built a motte and bailey castle; nothing can be seen of this today but it is believed to lie beneath the Mount Inn. Edward I gave the town a charter in 1280 and in 1344 it was made a self governing borough. Over the centuries different industries were responsible for bringing prosperity to Llanidloes: wool in the 16th; flannel in the 18th and 19th; lead mining and smelting in the 19th.

Today these industries are long

Top: The Old Market Hall; **Above left:** Llanidloes Museum in the Town Hall; **Above right:** Town Hall and the Market Hall in the background

gone but their legacy can be seen in the town's broad streets with many fine buildings. The old heart of the town was laid out in the form of a cross with the iconic Old Market Hall at the centre. This unusual structure is now home to the 'Celebration of Timber-framed Buildings' Exhibition. Numerous buildings of this type can be found around the town. Located in the Town Hall, Llanidloes museum has a useful local history gallery which gives a good introduction to the history and development of the town.

For many visitors however it will be the attractions of the great outdoors that brings them to this corner of Wales. Walkers will find an abundance of possible routes, with waymarked trails in Hafren

Forest and around Llyn Clywedog. Alternatively you could follow the Severn Way to the source high up on the bleak moorlands of Plynlimon. Cyclists will enjoy the varied terrain with traffic free routes offering wonderful views of mountains, lakes and forests. A recommended 18m/29km route visits Severn Break its Neck waterfall, Afon Biga picnic area and nature trail, the viewing area above the dam at Clywedog and the abandoned mine buildings at Bryn Tail. Bring your own bike or hire one locally.

Places to visit

Llanidloes Museum

Town Hall, Great Oak Street
SY18 6BN
☎ 01686 413777
The museum is a good starting place

for the visitor to discover the heritage of this small town. There are displays informing about the history of the Old Market Hall, the rise and fall of the mining and woollen industries and the intriguing story of the Chartist movement and its connection with Llanidloes.

Hafren Forest

This large forest, managed by the Forestry Commission, cloaks the eastern slopes of Plynlimon mountain. The lovely Rhyd-y-benwch picnic site, 6m/9km from Llanidloes, is the starting point for several marked walking trails of varying degrees of difficulty. Points of interest include waterfalls, old mines and the source of the river Severn.

Llyn Clywedog

Man made it may be but this wildly situated lake can lay claim to being one of the most beautiful in Wales. Six miles long and serpentine in shape it is a haven for birds such as red kites, buzzards, Canada geese, pied flycatchers and even the occasional sighting of an osprey. It's also a celebrated fly fishing venue; the local angling association annually releases 30,000 trout into its waters. Sailing is a popular pursuit on the 615 acres of water and the lake is open to all types of non-powered craft. There are several viewpoints around the lake and walkers will find a number of waymarked trails.

Attractions Nearby

Oriel Davies Gallery (13.5m/22km)

The Park, Newtown
SY16 2NZ
☎ 01686 625041
www.orieldavies.org
This striking modern building in the centre of Newtown houses exhibitions of modern Welsh and international art.

Hotels and Dining

Try the local Tourist Information Centre, see Essential Contacts for details.

Trewythen Hotel

Great Oak Street
SY18 6BW
☎ 01686 411333
www.trewythen.co.uk
A tastefully modernised grade II listed Georgian building in the centre of town, this hotel played a prominent part in the infamous Chartist riot in 1839. The pleasing modern restaurant is open to non-residents.

Red Lion

Longbridge Street
SY18 6EE
☎ 01686 412270
Family run and unpretentious, this traditional hotel is in the centre of town.

Lloyd's Hotel

Cambrian Place
SY18 6BX
☎ 01686 412284
www.lloydshotel.co.uk
Idiosyncratic guest house remodelled from a once larger hotel.

The Mount Inn

China Street
SY18 6AB
☎ 01686 412247
This one time coaching inn is a black and white half-timbered building on the site of a motte and bailey castle, hence the name. The building retains many original features such as oak beams and cobbled floors.

Maesmawr Hall Hotel (9m/14km)

Caersws
SY17 5SF
☎ 01686 688255
www.maesmawr.co.uk
Picturesque 17th century half timbered hall in countryside near the village of Caersws.

Grandstand B+B (4.5m/7km)

Trefeglwys, Caersws
SY17 5PV
☎ 01686 430491
www.grandstandbandb.co.uk
This five star rated B+B offers quality modern accommodation in a quiet country location with stunning views.

Bistro Hafren

2 Great Oak Street
SY18 6BN
☎ 01686 414936

Events

Sarn Sabrina Walk, a 24 mile challenge walk held in May.

Essential Briefing

Tourist Information Library

Mount Lane, Llanidloes
☎ 01686 412855

Theatr Hafran

Llanidloes Road, Newtown
SY16 4HU
☎ 01686 625007
www.theatrhafran.com

Hafren Cycle Hire

Capel Geufron, Old Hall
Llanidloes
SY18 6PT
☎ 01686 413565

Keep well clear of all old mines and buildings.

Getting There

By Road
The A487 runs north – south through the town. From the east it is approached along the A489.

By Rail
Machynlleth station is on the Birmingham to Aberystwyth line.

By Coach
To Aberystwyth then onward by local bus.

Left: The Memorial Clock, Machynlleth; **Right top:** Museum of Modern Art MOMA; **Right bottom:** Osprey viewing platform, A487 south of town

Background Briefing

The River Dyfi, which begins its life in a small pool beneath the towering cliffs of Aran Fawddwy, is often regarded as the natural boundary between north and south Wales. At the other end of the river the first road crossing is the narrow Dyfi Bridge, a few miles above the estuary near the town of Machynlleth. This historic market town with a population of around two thousand was granted a charter to hold a market way back in 1291; the tradition is still very much alive today with the main thoroughfare of Maengwyn Street packed with market stalls and shoppers every Wednesday.

A town with a strong sense of history, its people are proud of their association with Owain Glyndwr, the charismatic Welsh leader who, for a time, led a successful rebellion against the English King Henry IV. In 1404, with his cause in the ascendency, he summoned a Parliament in Machynlleth with representatives from the whole of Wales. The fascinating story of this episode in Welsh history can be discovered on a visit to the Owain Glyndwr Centre on Maengwyn Street.

The best known landmark in town is the Castlereagh Memorial Clock.

This imposing 78ft/24m high structure stands at the principal crossroad in the centre of town. It was built to commemorate the 21st birthday of Viscount Castlereagh, whose family seat was in Machynlleth; history does not record what the young man thought of his unusual birthday present.

The town today has a pleasing mix of buildings representing architectural styles over five centuries. The Royal House dates back to the 16th century and is so named because Charles I is said to have stayed there; it has been recently restored. The imposing neo-classical Tabernacle, once a Wesleyan chapel, is now home, along with adjacent buildings, to the Museum of Modern Art, Wales. The town has plenty of cafes and pubs plus an eclectic mix of independent shops.

There are lots of things to do in and around Mach, as it is known for short. Probably the best known attraction in the area is the Centre for Alternative Technology. This well established and ever changing site explains and demonstrates in an entertaining way how we can live in a more sustainable way; it represents a good day out for all the family and becomes more relevant with each passing day. There are numerous family friendly attractions in the area such as King Arthur's Labyrinth and Corris Narrow Gauge Railway. The beaches and other attractions of the Cambrian coast are all close at hand; why not travel by train on the Machynlleth to Pwllheli line, a scenic ride and a greener way to travel.

Places to visit

Owain Glyndwr Centre
Heol Maengwyn
SY20 8EE
☎ 01654 702932
www.canolfanowainglyndwrcentre
Learn about Owain Glyndwr's uprising and his links with Machynlleth, in particular the Parliament of 1404.

Museum of Modern Art, Wales (MOMA)
The Tabernacle, Heol Penrallt
SY20 8AJ
☎ 01654 703355
A centre for the visual and performing arts housed in a converted Weslyan chapel and adjoining buildings. Four galleries are used to display changing exhibitions by leading Welsh artists and a growing permanent collection. The 350 seat auditorium is home to the Machynlleth Festival and other events throughout the year.

Attractions Nearby

Centre for Alternative Technology (3m/5km)

Machynlleth
SY20 9AZ
☎ 01654 705959
www.cat.org.uk

Prepare to be educated, entertained and perhaps inspired by a visit to this renowned eco centre, now into its fourth decade. Everyone loves the cliff railway and the kids will find plenty of interactive displays and play areas to keep them amused.

Ynys Hir Nature Reserve (6.5m/10.5km)

Eglwys Fach
☎ 01654 70022

An extensive RSPB reserve with an impressive range of habitats; oak woodland, freshwater ponds and streams, saltmarsh, peat bogs and reed beds. The site covers over 1000 acres and there are seven hides, two nature trails and a visitor centre.

King Arthur's Labyrinth (5.5m/9km)

Corris Craft Centre, Corris
SY20 9RF
☎ 01654 761584
www.kingarthurslabyrinth.com

Explore the myth and legend of King Athur in the underground caverns of this atmospheric family orientated attraction. Also on the same site are the Bard's Quest maze and the craft centre with around a dozen craft studios.

Mountain Biking

The hilly terrain, often cloaked in forestry plantations, makes this ideal mountain biking country. There are three cross country routes of varying degrees of difficulty south of the town, following rights of way. There is also a purpose built trail north of the town in the Dyfi Forest. Ask at the tourist information centre or visit www.dyfi-mountainbiking.org.uk for more information.

Hotels and Dining

Try the local Tourist Information Centre, see Essential Contacts for details.

Something Special

Plas Dolguog Hotel

Felingerrig
SY20 8UJ
☎ 01654 702244
www.plasdolguog.co.uk

Beautifully situated in 9 acres of grounds and gardens overlooking the Dyfi valley just outside town. Well appointed accommodation in a historic manor house converted into a small hotel. The restaurant offers fine views over the valley towards the mountains.

Penmaendyfi (5.5m/9km)

Cwrt, Pennal
SY20 9LD
☎ 01654 791246
www.penmaendyfi.co.uk

Spacious bedrooms are a feature in this 16th century country mansion overlooking the Dyfi valley. Relax in front of a log fire in winter or by the outdoor pool in summer; there's a tennis court for the more energetic.

The White Lion Hotel

Heol Pentrehedyn
SY20 8DN
☎ 01654 703455
www.whitelionhotel.co.uk

Traditional coaching inn in the town centre with many original features. Dine in the restaurant, bar or garden.

Maenllwyd Guest House

Newtown Road
SY20 8EY
☎ 01654 702928
www.maenllwyd.co.uk

Comfortable B+B in one time manse near town centre with large garden and storage for bikes.

Ynyshir Hall Hotel (6.5m/10.5km)

Eglwysfach
SY20 8TA
☎ 01654781209
www.ynyshirhall.co.uk

A secluded luxury hotel on the southern shores of the Dyfi estuary set in 14 acres of mature garden. The bedrooms are individually designed and sumptuously furnished. The restaurant serves modern British cuisine, locally sourced.

Events

Machynlleth Festival

An annual festival of the arts held in August at the Tabernacle.
www.momawales.org.uk

Essential Contacts

Tourist Information Centre

Royal House
 Penrallt Street
SY20 8AG
☎ 01654 702401

Bike Hire

The Holey Trail
31 Maengwyn Street
SY20 8EB
☎ 01654 700411

Mountain bike courses and guided rides

Forest Freeride, Ceulan, Pennant
Llanbrynmair
SY19 7BH
☎ 01650 521301

Osprey Watch Visitors Centre

Just south of town on the A487. Observation hide and TV live-feed of the nest.

Mawddach Estuary, Gwynedd

Getting There

By Road

Dolgellau is on the A470 in the south west of the Snowdonia National Park.

By Rail

Barmouth is on the Cambrian line from Shrewsbury to Pwllheli.

By Coach

There are national coaches to Wrexham then the X94 service to Barmouth

Background Briefing

The Mawddach Estuary is a beautiful area encompassing Dolgellau, Fairbourne and Barmouth. It has

Top: Barmouth; Middle: Cymer Abbey; Bottom: Fairbourne Railway Station

walks for all, from gentle strolls to longer more strenuous hikes, all with magnificent scenery. There is bird watching with an RSPB Information Centre in the old signal box at Penmaenpool and the photo opportunities are endless.

An old market town in a majestic setting at the foot of Cader Idris, Dolgellau is a good base for exploring the area. It has many imposing listed buildings constructed of the local dolerite rock and slate, mostly dating back to the town's time as a centre for the area's woollen industry. An excellent Town Trail leaflet can be obtained from the TIC.

As well as the many routes to the summit of Cader Idris, there are other attractive walks from the town such as the Precipice Walk and Glyn Aran, both fairly short and giving panoramic views of the surrounding countryside. Coed y Brenin is only 7m/11km away with some fine mountain biking trails and if you prefer more leisurely cycling there is the Mawddach Trail, a 9m/14km stretch of former railway track from Dolgellau to Barmouth. The final stretch of this cycle ride is over the much photographed Barmouth railway bridge (no access to motor vehicles), a mainly wooden structure with lovely views of the estuary. Barmouth is an old shipbuilding town, now a popular seaside resort, on the estuary of the Mawddach River in the south west corner of Snowdonia National Park. It is a beautiful setting with a backdrop of mountains, a picturesque harbour and excellent Blue Flag beaches.

The beautiful sandy beach is extensive, with lots of room for games and sunbathing, so it never feels overcrowded. The old town is a jumble of steep terraces, paths and alleyways with many hidden corners to be explored. Above

the houses is Dinas Olau (Fortress of Light), the first piece of land owned by the National Trust; with a viewing point built to commemorate the Trust's centenary, it is part of Barmouth's famous Panorama Walk, which starts at the steps just before the railway bridge. On the quayside are several buildings of interest; for an insight into Barmouth's maritime past you can visit the Sailors Institute and Ty Gwyn a 15th century house with exhibitions about its history and Barmouth's seafaring past. Also on the quay is the RNLI's lifeboat museum and just behind the quay is a small round building which is the old lockup.

You can take the ferry from Barmouth to Penrhyn Point and catch the narrow gauge steam train to Fairbourne. Fairbourne is a small quiet seaside resort with a long sandy beach ideal for water sports such as wind surfing, canoeing, water skiing and of course sea fishing.

Places to visit

Quaker Heritage Centre

Ty Meirion, Sgwar Eldon
Dolgellau
☎ 01341 424680
Tells the story of the Quaker community that once lived here and of the persecution which forced them to emigrate to Pennsylvania.

Attractions Nearby

Coed y Brenin (7m/11km)

www.forestry.gov.uk/coed-y-breninforestpark
East of the A470, 8m/13km north of Dolgellau just north of Ganllwyd, south of Trawsfynydd. Follow the brown tourist signs.

Coed y Brenin has some of the best mountain biking trails in Wales with routes to suit all abilities. There are waymarked walking routes to suit all the family, a children's adventure playground, a cafe and bike shop where bikes can be hired.

Cymer Abbey (Cadw) (2m/3km)

Llanelltyd, Dolgellau
LL40 2HE

A small ruined abbey founded by the Cistercians in the 12th century, it is a remote and tranquil place at the head of the Mawddach Estuary.

Fairbourne Railway (9m/14.5km)

Beach Road, Fairbourne
LL38 2EX
☎ 01341 250362
www.fairbournerailway.com

This narrow gauge railway with its four steam engines runs from Fairbourne to Penrhyn Point from May to September. There is a ferry service from Penrhyn Point to Barmouth.

Hotels and Dining

Try the local Tourist Information Centre, see Essential Contacts for details.

Something Special

Penmaenuchaf Hall Hotel

Penmaenpool, Dolgellau
LL40 1YB
☎ 01341 422129
www.penhall.co.uk

A WTB 4 star luxury country house hotel with magnificent views over the Mawddach Estuary. The restaurant serving modern British food is AA 2 rosette rated.

Y Meirionnydd

Smithfield Square, Dolgellau
LL 40 1ES
☎ 01341 422554
www.themeirionnydd.com

A Georgian town house in the centre of town with bright comfortable rooms and a restaurant serving good food.

Ffynnon

Brynffynnon, Love Lane, Dolgellau
LL40 1RR
☎ 01341 421774
www.ffynnontownhouse.com

A WTB 5 star and gold award winning boutique style B & B offering luxurious modern comforts.

Plas Dolmelynllyn Country Hotel

Ganllwyd, Dolgellau
LL40 2HP
☎ 01341 440273
www.dolly-hotel.co.uk

Housed in an old Welsh manor house in several acres of gardens the hotel has an award winning restaurant.

Bae Abermaw Hotel

Panorama Hill, Barmouth
LL42 1DQ
☎ 01341 280 550
www.baeabermaw.com

WTB 4 star boutique coastal hotel and award winning restaurant with stunning views of the harbour and Cardigan Bay.

Ty'r Graig Castle

Llanaber Road, Barmouth
LL42 1YN
☎ 01341 280470
www.tyrgraigcastle.co.uk

The cliff top setting between the mountains and sea make this WTB 4 star rated hotel a little bit different.

The Bistro Restaurant

Church Street, Barmouth
LL42 1EW
☎ 01341 281284
www.bistro-barmouth.co.uk

An award winning restaurant that serves freshly cooked food using local produce.

Events

Sesiwn Fawr

www.sesiwnfawr.co.uk
Open air music festival held in July in Dolgellau.

Barmouth Walking Festival

September
www.barmouthwalkingfestival.co.uk

Barmouth Arts Festival

September

Essential Contacts

Dolgellau Tourist Information Centre

Ty Meirion, Eldon Square
LL40 1PU
Email: tic.dolgellau@eryri-npa.gov.uk
☎ 01341 422888

Dolgellau Town Trail Leaflet

www.civictrustwales.org/trails/Dolgellau/trail.html

Dolgellau Cycles (cycle hire)

The Old Furnace, Smithfield St.
LL40 1DF
☎ 01341 423332
www.dolgellaucycles.co.uk

Coed y Brenin Visitor Centre

Dolgefeilliau
☎ 01341 440747
www.forestry.gov.uk/coed-y-breninforestpark

Beics Brenin (cycle hire)

Coed Y Brenin Visitor Centre
Dolgefeiliau
LL40 2HZ
☎ 01341 440728
www.beicsbrenin.co.uk

Barmouth Tourist Information Centre

Station Road, Barmouth
LL42 1
☎ 01341 280787

Monmouth

By Road

Monmouth is on the A40 between Ross on Wye and Abergavenny.

By Rail

The nearest train stations are Abergavenny and Chepstow.

By Coach

There is one national coach per day to Monmouth.

Top: The gate tower, Monmouth; Middle: The Punch House, Monmouth; Bottom: Raglan Castle

Background Briefing

Monmouth is an interesting border town located at the confluence of three rivers - the Trothy, the Monnow and the Wye. It has a world famous and unique 14th century gate tower with portcullis, built to defend the 13th century Monnow Bridge. The town has some fine Tudor and Georgian buildings and the old coaching inns and Georgian Shire Hall in Agincourt Square make an elegant town centre. The narrow lanes of shops and attractive courtyards all add to the character of this bustling little town.

A visit to the Kymin, overlooking the town, gives magnificent views of both the town and surrounding countryside. Offa's Dyke path and the Wye Valley walk both pass through the town so walkers are well catered for. The Wye is famous for its salmon fishing as well as being a very scenic river and the Usk is also a beautiful river renowned for its salmon and trout fishing. Golfers too are well catered for with several golf clubs in or near the town.

It is a good base for exploring the surrounding area with the Brecon Beacons, the Wye Valley and the Forest of Dean all nearby.

A short journey to the south west is the small border town of Usk with its beautiful floral displays. It is a tranquil town now, with its ancient castle and bridge over the River Usk, but it has a long history and like most border towns has seen much fighting over the centuries between the English and the Welsh. Its rural museum is well worth a visit with something to keep all ages interested. Between Usk and Monmouth is the splendid Raglan Castle.

The Royal Forest of Dean is situated to the east of the town; it was the first area of woodland to be designated a national forest in 1939. An ancient woodland it has been used for hunting since Saxon times; these days it offers many outdoor activities from walking, cycling and rock climbing to canoeing and fishing. Symonds Yat Rock, a 500 foot limestone outcrop overlooking the River Wye, is a fine viewpoint and if you visit between April and August a pair of peregrine falcons may be seen nesting on the cliffs.

Places to visit

Nelson Museum

Priory Street, Monmouth
NP25 3XA
☎ 01600 710630

Monmouth has one of the world's best collections of Nelson memorabilia. The museum also features Charles Stuart Rolls, co-founder of Rolls-Royce, who lived near Monmouth and some local history exhibits.

The Kymin (NT)

The Round House, Monmouth
NP25 3SE
☎ 01600 719241

The Kymin is a wooded hill overlooking Monmouth topped by the Round House a Georgian banqueting house. It has 9 acres of pleasure grounds and as well as a panoramic view of the town, it has superb views of the Welsh countryside and mountains. There is also a Naval Temple in the grounds built by public subscription in 1800 in commemoration of the many naval victories in the late 18th century.

Attractions Nearby

Raglan Castle (Cadw) (9m/14 km)

Raglan, Usk, Monmouthshire
NP15 2BT
☎ 01291 690228
www.Cadw.wales.gov.uk

Raglan Castle was not built just as a fortress but as a statement of wealth and social aspiration. Started in 1435 it is one of the best medieval castles in the UK built as a lavish palace with formal apartments and a Great Gatehouse. The ruins are extensive and there is much to see of its former glory.

Usk Rural Life Museum (14m/23km)

The Malt Barn, New Market Street, Usk

NP15 1AU

☎ 01291 673777

www.uskmuseum.org.uk

Run by volunteers the museum has been described in a report on rural museums as "one of the best of its kind in Britain". It provides a great deal of information about rural life in Monmouthshire. It has a huge range of exhibits particularly covering the period from 1850 to the end of World War II. There is a typical farmhouse kitchen, a laundry and dairy, plus blacksmiths, cobblers and wheelwright's exhibits. There are many rural artefacts arranged by seasons and there is a collection of scale model horse-drawn vehicles. A fascinating visit for people of all ages.

Clearwell Caves (9miles/14km)

The Rocks, Clearwell

Coleford, Gloucestershire

GL16 8JR

☎ 01594 832535

www.clearwellcaves.com

Clearwell Caves are ancient iron ore mines dating as far back as Roman times. They are now a working mining museum where visitors can see nine caverns plus geological and mining displays, and a blacksmiths shop.

Hotels and Dining

Try the local Tourist Information Centre, see Essential Contacts for details.

Something Special

The Crown at Whitebrook (6m/10km)

Near Monmouth

NP25 4TX

☎ 01600 860254

www.crownatwhitebrook.co.uk

To the south of Monmouth the WTB 5 star Crown at Whitebrook retained its Michelin star for the 3rd year running in 2009. A restaurant with rooms, each unique room has luxurious contemporary styling and views of the beautiful countryside.

The Riverside Hotel

Cinderhill Street, Monmouth

NP25 5EY

☎ 01600 715577

www.riversidehotelmonmouth.co.uk

A friendly family run hotel situated by the ancient, fortified bridge over the River Monnow.

The Beaufort Arms Coaching Inn & Restaurant

High Street, Raglan Village

Monmouthshire

NP15 2DY

☎ 01291 690412

www.beaufortraglan.co.uk

This award winning 16th century coaching inn has been completely refurbished by the owners, to add elegance and comfort, whilst retaining its character.

The Stonemill (4m/6km)

Rockfield, Monmouth

NP25 5SW

☎ 01600 716273

www.thestonemill.co.uk

Set in a modernised 16th century barn the award winning Stonemill Restaurant offers excellent food and wine. It is listed in the Michelin Guide and the Which Good Food Guide and has 2 AA rosettes.

Events

Monmouth Festival

Music and entertainment festival at the end of July.

Essential Contact

Monmouth Tourist Information Centre

Market Hall; Priory Street

NP25 3XA

☎ 01600 713899

Monmouth Canoe & Activity Centre

Castle Yard, Old Dixton Road

Monmouth

NP25 3DP

☎ 01600 713461

www.monmouthcanoe.com

Pedalabikeaway Cycle Centre

Hadnock Road, Coleford

NP25 3NG

☎ 01600 772821

www.pedalabikeaway.co.uk

Porthmadog, Gwynedd

Getting There

By Road
From the M6 take the M56 and then the A55 to Bangor. The A487 from Bangor passes through Porthmadog.

By Rail
Porthmadog is on the Cambrian Coast Railway, change at Machynlleth or Shrewsbury.

By Coach
National Coaches go to Porthmadog.

Background Briefing

Porthmadog is a busy small town at the northern end of Cardigan Bay where it turns the corner westwards to the Lleyn Peninsula. Unlike most towns in Wales it does not have a long history being developed by W A Madocks in the early 1800s. The town's early prosperity was based on the transportation of slate, from the quarries at Blaenau Ffestiniog around the world, from the busy harbour and the associated ship building in the area.

These days the town is a thriving tourist destination being well placed as a base to explore Snowdonia National Park, with its rugged mountains and splendid scenery, whilst in contrast the Lleyn Peninsula offers gentler countryside and a stunning coastline. The Mediterranean style holiday village of Portmeirion is nearby and two of the best of Edward I's castles, Harlech and Caernarfon are within easy driving distance.

The town has lots of individual shops and even its own department store and there are lots of places for the visitor to eat out. The Ffestiniog and West Highland narrow gauge railways are a big attraction to visi-

Top: Porthmadog Harbour
Above: Criccieth Castle

tors and the harbour, with its views of the estuary and mountains, is a pleasant place to sit and watch the world go by. A one mile walk past the yacht club and boatyards over the hill brings you to Borth y Gest, a charming quiet seaside village, with panoramic views across the Glaslyn Estuary second to none. It has attractive sandy coves and the estuary is a great place for bird watching. To the west of Porthmadog is Black Rock Sands, a two mile stretch of sandy beach on to which you can drive your car. There is lots of space for all beach activities and sports and being so large you need never feel crowded.

A short journey west brings you to the small resort of Criccieth with the castle on its promontory separating the town's two beaches. It has everything you need in a resort, accommodation, cafes, ice cream, a sandy beach with rock pools and a slipway to launch sail boats and kayaks and of course wonderful views.

Places to visit

Ffestiniog Railway
Ffestiniog & Welsh Highland Railways, Harbour Station Porthmadog
LL49 9NF
☎ 01766 516000
www.ffestiniograilway.co.uk
The world famous 2ft gauge steam railway takes you on a 13½m/22km journey from the harbour in Porthmadog to the slate-quarrying town of Blaenau Ffestiniog.

Welsh Highland Railway
Ffestiniog & Welsh Highland Railways, Harbour Station Porthmadog
LL49 9NF
☎ 01766 516000
www.welshhighlandrailway.net
This narrow gauge railway is due to link up to the Ffestiniog Railway in 2011. You will then be able to make a trip of 40m/64km from Blaenau Ffestiniog via Porthmadog to Caernarfon through some of Wales' most spectacular scenery.

Porthmadog Maritime Museum
Oakley Wharf No 1
The Harbour, Porthmadog
LL49 9LU
☎ 01766 513736
One of the old slate sheds is the home to the small maritime museum. There are models, pictures, documents and tools illustrating the importance of ship building to Porthmadog.

Attractions Nearby

Portmeirion (3m/5km)
Minffordd, Penrhyndeudraeth
LL48 6ER
☎ 01766 770000
www.portmeirion-village.com
Portmeirion Italianate village designed by Clough Williams-Ellis is set on its own headland about 2.5

miles south east of Porthmadog. The village is a top visitor attraction in North Wales and as well as its many buildings, mainly holiday accommodation, it has extensive grounds and gardens. It was made famous in the late sixties as the location for the TV series *The Prisoner*.

Beddgelert (8m/12.5km)

To the north is the pretty village of Beddgelert set at the foot of mount Snowdon. The beautiful River Glaslyn runs through the village before it flows down the rocky much photographed Aberglaslyn Pass. The village church St Mary's stands on a religious site that has been occupied since the 6th century, it still has the remains of medieval features although it was much restored in Victorian times. The oldest building in the village, a 17th century farm house Ty Isaf, houses a shop and exhibition about the history and wildlife of the area. Finally on the outskirts of the village is the Sygun Copper Mine with audio visual tours available.

Sygun Copper Mine (8m/12.5km)

Beddgelert
LL55 4NE
☎ 01766 89059
www.syguncoppermine.co.uk
The audio visual tour guides you round the old 19th century workings and explains the mining processes. You can see stalactites and stalagmites formed from ferrous oxide and the copper ore veins with their traces of precious metals.

Harlech Castle (Cadw) (10m/16km)

Castle Square, Harlech
LL46 2YH
☎ 01766 780552
A World Heritage Site this castle built by Edward Ist is probably one of the most spectacular, perched on a cliff, it dominates the area.

Hotels and Dining

Try the local Tourist Information Centre, see Essential Contacts for details.

Something Special

Glyn y Coed Hotel

Portmadog Rd. Criccieth
LL52 0HP
☎ 01766 522870
www.glynycoedhotel.co.uk
As well as WTB 5 stars and Gold Host award the Glyn-y-Coed has also been awarded Red Diamonds from the AA and a Sparkling Diamond Award from the RAC. The newly refurbished hotel is on the seafront with unrivalled views of Cardigan Bay, the castle and mountains.

Plas Tan-Yr-Allt

Tremadog
LL49 9RG
☎ 01766 514 545
www.tanyrallt.co.uk
In the Good Hotel Guide the country house hotel Plas Tan-Yr-Alt offers luxury B & B accommodation, situated in 47 acres of grounds overlooking the Glaslyn Estuary.

Mynydd Ednyfed Country House Hotel

Caernarfon Road, Criccieth
LL52 0PH UK
☎ 01766 523269
A WTB 3 star family-run country house hotel, set in 7 acres of gardens and woodlands, with views of Cardigan Bay and Criccieth Castle. This 400 year old house offers modern style and comfort in a tranquil setting.

The Royal Sportsman Hotel

131 High Street, Porthmadog
LL49 9HB
☎ 01766 512 490
www.royalsportsman.co.uk

AA and WTB 3 star hotel in the centre of Porthmadog. Recently refurbished the hotel prides itself on its old fashioned service, hospitality and a personal approach. The award winning chefs produce a varied menu using locally sourced ingredients.

Grapevine Bistro

152 High Street, Porthmadog
LL49 9NU
☎ 01766 514230
www.grapevinebistrorestaurant.co.uk

Moorings Bistro

4 Ivy Terrace, Borth y Gest
LL49 9TS
☎ 01766 513500
www.mooringsbistroborthygest.com

Events

Criccieth Festival – June
www.cricciethfestival.co.uk

Top: Festiniog Railway; **Bottom:** Portmeirion

Ruthin, Denbighshire

Top: Ruthin; Above: Denbigh Castle

Background Briefing

The Vale of Clwyd, with its rich verdant pasture land, lies between the Clwydian Range of hills and the high plateau of Denbigh Moors; towards its head lies the charming historic town of Ruthin.

Today Ruthin is a peaceful place, a tourist destination where visitors can relax and unwind from the pressures of 21st century urban life. It hasn't always been quiet here though throughout its history. In 1400 it suffered the misfortune of seeing the first hostilities in Owain Glyndwr's great revolt. Glyndwr, from the neighbouring Dee Valley, had a grievance against the incumbent of Ruthin castle, the Baron de Grey which resulted in Glydwr and his supporters attacking Ruthin and burning most of it to the ground. The castle was one of the few buildings to survive this assault. Moving forward a couple of centuries the castle saw action in the civil war when the Royalist garrison was besieged by Parliamentary forces for eleven weeks. They were eventually compelled to surrender and Parliament then ordered the dismantling of the castle. It remained in ruins until in the 19th century the present mansion was constructed around the remains.

Today's visitor to Ruthin can see examples of buildings spanning six centuries, on a street pattern dating from medieval times. Ruthin has more listed buildings than any other market town in North Wales and several are to be found in St Peter's Square, the hub of the town, and a good place to sit and soak up the atmosphere. The half timbered Old Court House, now a bank, features the remains of the gibbet, last used in 1679. Another interesting building is the Myddleton Arms; this 16th century inn has a remarkable roof which because of the unusual arrangement of windows has come to be known as 'the eyes of Ruthin'.

Attractions to visit in the town include Nantclwyd y Dre, Wales' oldest timber framed house, the museum of prison life at the Old Gaol, and the recently reconstructed Ruthin Craft Centre. The surrounding countryside is a great place for country walks; try Moel Fammau the highest peak in the Clwydian range, Loggerheads for its superb limestone scenery or Llyn Brenig for a walk round the lake. The more adventurous may like to try abseiling into Devil's Gorge at Loggerheads or mountain biking in Llandegla Forest. In the evening you could travel the short distance to Clwyd Theatr Cymru in Mold to enjoy a play or film.

Places to visit

Nantclwyd y dre
Castle Street
LL15 1DP
☎ 01824 709822

A splendid timber framed building dating from 1435. Recently restored the seven rooms each represent a different period in the house's history. It even has a resident colony of bats, whose activities can be followed on the 'bat cam'.

Ruthin Craft Centre
Park Road
LL15 1BB
☎ 01824 704774
www.ruthincraftcentre.org.uk

An exciting new development showcasing the talents of craftsmen from Britain and around the world. The striking new building houses galleries, workshops, shop and café.

Ruthin Gaol
Clwyd Street
LL15 1HP
☎ 01824 708281

For something a bit different try a visit to Ruthin Gaol for a fascinating, if rather grim, exploration of life as a 19th century prisoner.

Attractions Nearby

Bodelwyddan Castle (17m/27km)
Bodelwyddan
LL18 5YA
☎ 01745 584060
www.bodelwyddan-castle.co.uk

Fine art treasures from the National Portrait Gallery housed in lavishly restored Victorian mansion. The house is set in 260 acres of parkland with formal gardens and extensive woodland walks.

St Asaph Cathedral (13m/21km)
High Street, St Asaph
LL17 0RD
☎ 01745 583429

Although there has been a church on this site since the 6th century the present building is based on a 14th century core. A turbulent history has resulted in a need for several rebuilds so the current structure is a pleasant amalgam of various styles from different centuries. Despite its modest proportions it's well worth a visit; look out for the William Morgan Bible, the first Bible to be published in the Welsh language in 1588.

Llyn Brenig (27m/43km)
Llyn Brenig Visitor Centre
Cerrigydrudion
LL21 9TT
☎ 01490420463

Blow away the cobwebs on a visit to Llyn Brenig, a beautifully situated stretch of water, actually a reservoir, high on the Denbigh Moors. If you're feeling energetic try the 10 mile round the lake walk. More leisurely walks are available, including an archaeology trail. Facilities include a café, picnic areas and an adventure playground.

Moel Fammau (3m/5km)
Stay in Ruthin and you will feel the pull of the Clwydian hills, modest in height but splendid in form, serenely spanning the eastern horizon. The highest and nearest of these hills to Ruthin is Moel Fammau. It is possible to walk from the town, or take the car to the pass of Bwlch Pen Barras. The peak is topped by the remains of the Jubilee Tower, built to celebrate the golden jubilee of George III but never actually completed; now the rugged base provides a platform to admire the extensive views, including on a clear day Blackpool Tower and the Isle of Man.

Hotels and Dining
Try the local Tourist Information Centre, see Essential Contacts for details.

Something Special
Ruthin Castle Hotel
Castle Road
LL15 2NU
☎ 01483 776344
www.ruthincastle.co.uk

Victorian opulence with modern amenities in a grand 19th century building constructed in red sandstone around the remains of the medieval castle. Renowned for its medieval banquets; see the website for dates.

Manorhaus
Well Street
LL15 1AH
www.manorhaus.com

Contemporary style with individually designed bedrooms located within a listed Georgian townhouse.

Landmark Trust
Dolbelydr, nr Trefnant
Elegant manor, built in 1579, sleeps up to 6.
Monkton Old Hall, Monkton
14th century guest house of a small priory, sleeps up to 7.

Ye Olde Anchor Inn
Rhos Street
LL15 1DY
☎ 01824 702813

Oak beams, open fires and old world charm are on offer at this historic town centre inn.

Eyarth Station (1.5m/2.5km)
Llanfair Dyffryn Clwyd
LL15 2EE
☎ 01824 703643
www.eyarthstation.com

Comfortable B+B in converted old rural railway station, with small swimming pool.

Rhydonnen (5m/8km)
Llanychan
LL15 1UG
☎ 01824 790258
www.rhydonnen.co.uk

This fine 15th century black and white timbered house in a quiet corner of the Vale of Clwyd offers quality B+B in a house full of original architectural features.

Events
Ruthin Festival A full week of music, featuring jazz, classical, folk, pop and international at this annual festival, held in July. www.ruthinfestival.co.uk

South Ceredigion

Getting There

By Road

From the south take the M4 to Carmarthen, then take the A484 north to the Teifi Valley.

From the north head for Aberystwyth and then take the A487 to Cardigan.

By Rail

Carmarthen and Aberystwyth are the nearest railway stations, then onward by local bus.

By Coach

National coaches to Carmarthen or Aberystwyth then onward by local bus.

Above: Cardigan town centre

Background Briefing

South Ceredigion from Aberporth round the Teifi estuary to Cardigan and up the Teifi Valley to Lampeter is an ideal area for a short, away from it all break. The River Teifi, thought by many to be the most beautiful in Wales, passes through rolling hills and meadows with a network of footpaths and a series of small market towns to explore. The river is world famous for its fishing, with sewin (sea trout), salmon and wild brown trout plus plentiful coarse fishing too.

Lampeter or Llanbedr Pont Steffan in Welsh, is a small market town with the oldest university in Wales and arguably the third oldest in England and Wales after Oxford and Cambridge. You can stroll through the grounds of the University with its neo-gothic style old building, modelled on the Oxford quadrangle. It is surprisingly cosmopolitan for such a small town with a wide variety of shops. It has an annual food festival with over 60 stalls to promote local and organic food.

Above: Cardigan Heritage Centre

A few miles down river is Newcastle Emlyn, another small friendly market town at the heart of the Teifi Valley, with an excellent choice of shops, pubs and eating places. Legend says it was here that the last dragon in Wales was killed on the castle walls! The grounds of the ruined 13th century castle next to the River Teifi are an excellent place for a picnic. Close to the town at Dre-fach Felindre is the National Wool Museum and the Teifi Valley narrow gauge steam railway is also nearby, running for 2m/3km from Henllan to Llandyfriog.

Continuing downstream, Cenarth is a pretty conservation village with its many tumbling waterfalls and salmon leaps, a 17th century flour mill and a 200 year old bridge with intriguing cylindrical holes in its structure. The National Coracle Centre is situated in the grounds of the old mill with exhibitions and demonstrations of coracle building and sailing. The coracle is a small, shallow boat with a basketwork frame, propelled by a paddle; they are still used on the River Teifi today.

Castle Cilgerran, set in woods at the edge of a steep gorge on the river, is famous as the place where in 1109 Nest, the Welsh 'Helen of Troy' was abducted by Owain, son of the prince of Powys, an act which plunged the nation into war.

Cilgerran is home to the Teifi Marshes Nature Reserve with its stunning visitor centre.

Cardigan is an ancient Welsh cultural and commercial centre on the Teifi estuary. The town is full of Georgian and Victorian buildings, traditional shops, inns and places to eat, all helping create a charming nostalgic atmosphere. Many of the facades of the town centre shops have recently been restored and the quayside has been rebuilt with a new civic area and landing stage.

At the mouth of the River Teifi, Gwbert has some magnificent views out towards Cardigan Island and Poppit Sands.

On the coast 7m/11km from Cardigan, just north of the Teifi Estuary, is the attractive little resort of Aberporth. It has two safe, sandy, blue flag beaches with rock pools that are exposed at low tides, making it popular with families as well as divers and the boating fraternity. The cliff top walks along the Ceredigion Coast Path offer extensive views and opportunities for wildlife spotting. Bottlenose dolphins are seen frequently close to shore and sunfish and basking sharks are often seen offshore in the summer.

Places to visit

Gerddi Cae Hir Gardens & tea room

Cribyn, Lampeter
SA48 7NG
☎ 01570 470839
www.caehirgardens.ws
Open April to November
An original modern garden created by Wil Akkermans using both exotic and native plants.

National Wool Museum

Dre-fach Felindre
Near Newcastle Emlyn
Llandysul, Carmarthenshire
SA44 5UP
☎ 01559 370929
www.museumwales.ac.uk/en/wool

Above left: Gerddi Cae Hir Gardens; **Above right:** National Wool Museum

Dre-fach Felindre, also known as the 'Huddersfield of Wales' was once the centre of the Welsh woollen industry, with over 40 mills in the area at its peak. Part of the National Museum of Wales, all aspects of this traditional industry of woollen production are covered. There is also a working mill in production on site.

Teifi Valley Railway

Henllan Station
Henllan
Newcastle Emlyn
SA44 5TD
☎ 01559 370077
www.narrow-gauge-pleasure.co.uk/rlyteifi.html

Above: Teifi Valley Railway

National Coracle Centre

Cenarth Falls, Newcastle Emlyn
Carmarthenshire
SA38 9JL
☎ 01239 710 980
www.coracle-centre.co.uk
The National Coracle Centre, housed beside the beautiful Cenarth Falls, has coracles from all over the world on display. An exhibition of the ancient craft of coracle making can be seen in the workshop. Coracles can be seen on the river and rides are sometimes available.
Open from Easter to the end of October.

Welsh Wildlife Centre

Cilgerran, Cardigan
SA43 2TB
☎ 01239 621600
www.welshwildlife.org/wwcIntro_en.link
The Welsh Wildlife Centre is an impressive glass and timber building on the Teifi Marshes Nature Reserve. It has an interactive indoor display of local natural and social history about the River Teifi and Cilgerran. The adventurous can take a canoe trip up river as far as Cilgerran Castle.

Top: The old bridge at Cenarth
Above: Coracle, Cenarth

Cardigan Heritage Centre

Teifi Wharf, Castle Street
Cardigan
SA43 3AA
☎ 01239 614404
The history of Cardigan from pre-Norman times to the present day is displayed in this 18th century warehouse, with static and interactive computer displays. There is also a riverside cafe and craft shop.

Cardigan Island Coastal Farm Park

Gwbert, Cardigan
SA43 1PR
☎ 01239 623637
www.cardiganisland.co.uk
An island nature reserve with dramatic cliffs and clear blue sea. You may see bottlenose dolphins, Atlantic grey seals, seal pups, harbour porpoises, sea-birds, rare choughs and skylarks.

Attractions Nearby

Dolaucothi Roman Gold Mines (NT) (9m/14 km from Lampeter)

Pumsaint, Llanwrda
Carmarthenshire
SA19 8US
☎ 01558 825146
Visitors can sieve for gold, or don a miners' helmet to take a guided tour of the underground workings. There is a visitor centre, shop and cafe all set in a country estate with fantastic scenery.

Hotels and Dining

Try the local Tourist Information Centre, see Essential Contacts for details.

Something special

Cliff Hotel and Spa

Gwbert, Cardigan
SA43 1PP
☎ 01239 613241
www.cliffhotel.com
Newly refurbished this AA 3 star hotel offers luxury accommodation on the Pembrokeshire Heritage Coastline. The restaurant is Egon Ronay recommended. Facilities include a golf course and modern spa with body and beauty treatments.

Falcondale Mansion Hotel

Falcondale Drive, Lampeter
SA48 7RX
☎ 01570 422910
www.bw-falcondalemansion.co.uk
A 150 year old mansion set in 14 acres of woodland and garden just 1 mile from Lampeter.

Maes-y-Derw

Newcastle Emlyn,
Carmarthenshire
SA38 9RD
☎ 01239 710860
www.maes-y-derw.co.uk
A small 5 star B&B in an impressive Edwardian house on the edge of Newcastle Emlyn.

Castell Malgwyn Hotel

Llechryd, Cardigan
SA43 2QA
☎ 01239 682382
www.castellmalgwyn.co.uk/
A 3 star Georgian mansion set in tranquil countryside. It has a mile of fly fishing which is free to residents.

Landmark Trust

Church Cottage, Llandygwydd
The first Landmark, acquired in 1965, sleeps up to 4.

Events

Lampeter Food Festival

Cilgerran Coracle Races

Cardigan River and Food Festival

Cardigan Festival of Walking

Essential Contacts

Cardigan Tourist Information Centre Theatr Mwldan

Bath House Road, Cardigan
SA43 1JY
☎ 01239 613230
Theatr Mwldan is a vibrant arts and entertainment complex, situated in the centre of Cardigan, which also houses the TIC.

Heritage Canoes

☎ 01239 623633
For canoe trips from the Welsh Wildlife Centre.

Llandysul Angling Association

www.fishing-in-wales.com
For fishing permits along the Teifi.

Getting There

By Road

Llanwrtyd Wells, Llangammarch Wells, Builth Wells and Llandrindod Wells are served by the A483 Newtown to Swansea road.

By Rail

Llanwrtyd Wells, Llangammarch Wells and Llandrindod Wells have stations on the Swansea to Shrewsbury line. The station at Builth Road is 2m/3km from Builth Wells.

By Coach

Coach to Newtown then local bus.

Background Briefing

For more than half a century from the mid 1860s the area bounded by Llanwrtyd Wells in the south to Llandrindod Wells in the north experienced a period of unprecedented prosperity, thanks to the popularity of 'taking the waters' at spa resorts. Industrial workers from the South Wales valleys, middle class people from the Midlands, they all flocked on the newly built railways to the rapidly expanding inland resorts of Mid Wales.

The Victorian and Edwardian visitors came to drink the medicinal waters and enjoy the fresh country air and magnificent scenery of the region and also to engage in outdoor pursuits such as walking, shooting and fishing. Today, although no-one comes to take the waters, the area still welcomes visitors who delight in country activities; and the spa experience in its modern form can be experienced in several of the local hotels. Popular activities in the area include walking, cycling, fishing, golf, pony trekking and clay pigeon shooting.

Top: Llandrindod Wells
Middle: Llanwrtyd Wells
Bottom: Llangammach Wells

Llanwrtyd Wells, with its proximity to the great wilderness of the Elenydd is a good place for challenging walking and mountain biking. Pony trekking is popular here with riders enjoying magnificent views as they pass through woodland and over rugged moorland. It is also a centre for more unusual activities, often bizarre and extreme, perhaps the most well known being the curious pursuit of bog snorkelling. See the events section for the busy programme of events at this lively small town.

Nearby Llangammarch Wells, a village at the confluence of the rivers Cammarch and Irfon, is the quietest of the former spa resorts. It's the perfect hideaway, well away from traffic and light pollution; try gazing at the Milky Way on a starlit night.

At Builth Wells you can enjoy the laid back atmosphere in the friendly old market town with its numerous small shops or take a ramble along the Wye Valley Way as it follows the river upstream towards Newbridge.

Llandrindod Wells is a place to relax and unwind as you stroll in the parks, admire the elegance of the Victorian buildings, or enjoy a leisurely walk to nearby beauty spots. Alternatively why not take a trip on the scenic Heart of Wales railway line to the historic cathedral city of Shrewsbury.

Places to visit

National Cycle Collection

The Automobile Palace
Temple Street, Llandrindod Wells
LD1 5DL
☎ 01597 825531
www.cyclemuseum.org.uk
The evolution of the bicycle from the Penny Farthing to the latest models.

Cambrian Woollen Mill

Llanwrtyd Wells
LD5 4SD
☎ 01591 610363
Discover how cloth is made from the shearing of sheep through spinning and weaving to finishing at one of the few remaining woollen mills in Wales.

Radnorshire Museum

Temple Street, Llandrindod Wells
LD1 5DL
☎ 01597 824513
Tells the story of the development of the spa.

Hotels and Dining

Try the local Tourist Information Centre, see Essential Contacts for details.

Something Special

Lake Country House Hotel and Spa

Llangammach Wells
LD4 4BS
☎ 01591 620202
www.lakecountryhouse.co.uk
Relax and be pampered in this luxury country house hotel dating back to 1840 but fully brought up to date with sumptuously decorated rooms, a wide range of health and beauty treatments, indoor pool and balcony hot tub. Outdoors there are 50 acres of parkland sweeping down to the river Irfon and a lake well stocked with trout. Fishing breaks are a speciality.

Caer Beris Manor Hotel

Builth Wells
LD2 3NP
☎ 01982 552601
www.caerberis.com
Historic manor house in 27 acres of parkland on the edge of town. The hotel is lavishly furnished and it caters for a wide variety of outdoor activities.

Neuadd Arms Hotel

The Square, Llanwrtyd Wells
LD5 4RB
☎ 01591 610236
www.neuaddarmshotel.co.uk
Conveniently located traditional inn with 21 rooms and its own micro brewery.

Plas Newydd B+B

Irfon Terrace, Llanwrtyd Wells
LD5 4RH
☎ 01591 610293
www.plasnewydd90.co.uk
Award winning B+B with attractive garden.

Metropole Hotel

Temple Street, Llandrindod Wells
LD1 5DY
☎ 01597 823700
www.metropole.co.uk
Grand hotel in the centre of town with indoor pool, sauna and steam room.

Carlton Riverside Restaurant

Irfon Crescent, Llanwrtyd Wells
LD5 4ST
www.carltonrestaurant.co.uk
Award winning, contemporary styled restaurant plus bistro located near the town centre.

Events

Llanwrtyd Wells:

www.green-events.co.uk

World Bog Snorkelling Championship

Increasingly popular weird race in which competitors swim 120yds/109m through a trench cut in a peat bog wearing flippers and snorkel.

Man versus Horse Marathon

Established in 1980 this race over a hilly 22 mile course through some of the finest scenery in Mid Wales pits runner against horse rider.

Other events, held throughout the year, include mountain biking and walking activities and even a music and dance festival.

Builth Wells:

Royal Welsh Show
Wales' premier agricultural show held annually in July at the permanent showground just outside the town. Other shows held on the site include the Winter Fair and the Smallholder and Garden Festival.
www.rwas.co.uk

Llandrindod Wells:

Victorian Festival
Heart of Wales Walking Festival

Essential Contacts

Tourist Information Offices

Ty Barcud

The Square, Llanwrtyd Wells
LD5 4RB
☎ 01591 610666

Groe Car Park

Builth Wells
LD2 3BL
☎ 01982 553307

The Automobile Palace

Llandrindod Wells
LD1 5HU
☎ 01597 822600

Ffos Farm Riding Centre

Ffos Road, Llanwrtyd Wells
LL5 4RS
☎ 01591 610459
www.ffosfarm.co.uk
Pony trekking for all levels of ability.

Heart of Wales Railway

www.heart-of-wales.co.uk

St. Davids, Pembrokeshire

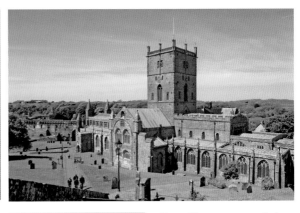

Getting There

By Road
St Davids is on the A487 between Haverfordwest and Fishguard.

By Rail
The nearest station is Haverfordwest and then local bus.

By Coach
National coaches go to Haverford-west and then local bus.

Background Briefing

St Davids, officially the smallest city in the UK, is really a most appealing village. Set in the Pembrokeshire Coast National Park, on a headland at the south west corner of Wales, it has spectacular coastal scenery, magnificent beaches and abundant wildlife. The star attraction of the city is its cathedral constructed of blue Cambrian sandstone and the adjacent bishop's palace ruins.

Although small St Davids visitors are well catered for and there are several award winning restaurants. In September there is an annual festival that celebrates food and countryside crafts with cookery demonstrations, tastings, local foods and crafts.

The city has a thriving artists' community and there are several galleries in and around St Davids you can visit.

Oriel y Parc, the new National Park Visitor Centre, has much of interest to the visitor. It has world-class galleries exhibiting art and artefacts from the National Museum of Wales collection, work by famous 20th century artist Graham Sutherland, and an artist in residence studio. There is an interactive interpretation area which explains what you can see and do during your visit to the National Park and

Top: St Davids Cathedral
Above: The Bishop's Palace

it is also the Tourist Information Centre for St Davids.

The city is a good place to stay for those who want a more energetic break with companies offering tuition and equipment hire for such activities as sea kayaking, surfing, wind surfing, climbing and coasteering.

Walkers are well catered for as the Pembrokeshire Coastal Path with its breathtaking scenery, carpets of wild flowers in the springtime and abundant wildlife, passes within a mile of the city. Other walks can include the beautiful Whitesands Bay or St Nons well and chapel, reputedly the site of the birth of St David, on the cliff top. You can visit the Iron Age Fort on St Davids Head or explore the Neolithic burial chamber, Coetan Arthur. There are several leaflets with these and other walks in the area available from National Park Visitor

Centre. There are many quiet lanes and roads in the area ideal for the leisure cyclist and bikes can be hired in St Davids.

There are boat trips to see the wildlife such as whales and dolphins, an evening puffin and shearwater cruise and trips to Ramsey Island, which can include a day walk with an RSPB warden as guide.

Places to visit

St Davids Cathedral
The Close
St Davids
SA62 6RH
☎ 01437 720199/720204
www.stdavidscathedral.org.uk
St Davids Cathedral sits in a grassy hollow on the site of a monastery founded by St David, patron saint of Wales. Building of the cathedral was started about 1180, although the building you see today has been altered, extended and restored over the subsequent centuries. When you enter the cathedral and walk up the central aisle the first thing you notice is you are walking up hill, indeed the from the east end of the building to the west the difference is about 13ft/4m. A place of pilgrimage for many centuries the cathedral is still a place of worship offering peace and tranquility for all who visit.

Bishops Palace (Cadw)

The bishop's palace is next door to the cathedral; even as a ruin it is an imposing building and when it was built in the 13th / 14th centuries it must have been truly impressive, with no expense spared on its construction. It has two sets of state rooms and a great hall with a striking wheel window plus private chambers, kitchens and chapel.

Attractions Nearby

Ramsey Island (RSPB)

Thousand Islands Expeditions
Cross Square, St. Davids
☎ 01437 721721
www.thousandislands.co.uk
With magnificent views of the Pembrokeshire coast from its rocky hills, a boat trip to the RSPB's Ramsey Island is a treat not to be missed. There is of course an abundance of bird life to be seen on the island including choughs, peregrines, shearwaters, guillemots, ravens, razorbills and many more. The carpets of bluebells, thrift and heather are a splendid sight from May to September and a colony of grey seals can be seen in September.

Boat trips are available to the

Top: Whitesands Bay at sunset
Above: Newgale

island from 1st April or Easter to the end of October from St Justinian's harbour.

Hotels and Dining

Try the local Tourist Information Centre, see Essential Contacts for details.

Something Special

Ramsey House

Lower Moor, St Davids
SA62 6RP
☎ 01437 720321 or 0779 557 5005
www.bandbstdavids.co.uk
Refurbished in a luxury boutique style Ramsey House is WTB 5 stars and AA 5 gold stars and Highly Commended. It also has AA awards for its breakfasts and dinners.

Landmark Trust

Tower Hill
Adjacent to the cathedral, sleeps up to 6.

Warpool Court Hotel

St Davids
SA62 6BN
☎ 01437 720300
www.warpoolcourthotel.com
This AA 3 star hotel has the coveted AA 2 rosette award for its food. Set in lawned gardens it has views of St Brides Bay and the offshore islands.

The Grove Hotel

High Street, St Davids
SA62 6SB
☎ 01437 720341
www.grovestdavids.co.uk
Set in a landscaped walled garden near the cathedral the restaurant at this hotel offers fine dining plus a bar menu, with all the old favourites, and a light bites menu too.

Cwtch

22 High Street, St Davids
SA62 6SD
☎ 01437 720491

www.cwtchrestaurant.co.uk
Award winning restaurant in the middle of St Davids. It advertises food that is good and honest with ingredients that are fresh, delicious and locally sourced. Cwtch is in the 2009 Michelin Red Guide and the 2009 Good Food Guide.

Morgans Brasserie

20 Nun Street, St Davids
SA62 6NT
☎ 01437 720508
www.morgans-in-stdavids.co.uk
This restaurant has an intimate atmosphere and exciting menus. There is a strong emphasis on locally sourced food. It has AA 2 rosettes and features in both the Good Food guide 2009 and the AA Restaurant Guide 2009.

Events

St Davids Cathedral Festival

May/June
www.stdavidscathedral.org.uk

Really Wild Food and Countryside Festival

September
www.reallywildfestival.co.uk

Essential Contacts

National Park Visitor Centre

Oriel y Parc, The Grove
St Davids
SA62 6NW
☎ 01437 720392
www.orielyparc.co.uk

For coasteering, kayaking, rock climbing and surfing

TYF Adventure

1 High Street, St Davids
SA62 6SA
☎ 01437 721611
www.tyf.com

Swansea

Getting There

By Road
The A483 from junction 42 of the M4 leads directly to the city centre.

By Rail
Swansea rail station is in the centre of the city and is served by through trains from London, Cardiff and Manchester.

By Coach
There are regular coach services into Swansea Bus Station.

Background Briefing

Swansea, sitting on the five mile sweep of Swansea Bay, is Wales' second largest city. It has an intimate relationship with the sea that has over the centuries been pivotal in its success. In medieval times it was a flourishing trading port. During the industrial revolution the port was crucial in the development of the metallurgical industries which brought it much wealth. Now the heavy industry has gone and the re-development of the redundant docks has become the focus of a vigorous re-invention of the city's role.

The new Maritime Quarter is the home to an ever expanding yachting marina and several top notch tourist attractions such as the National Waterfront Museum, the Dylan Thomas Centre, the LC centre, Swansea Museum and Plantasia. This area is a good place to start your visit; take a walk round the marina, admiring the moored yachts and the preserved boats belonging to Swansea Museum before deciding which of the attractions to try. You could immerse yourself in the interactive displays at the Waterfront Museum to learn the inspiring story of technical innovation through the

Top: Swansea Marina; Above: Dylan Thomas sculpture

ages, or wander through the galleries in the more traditionally presented Swansea Museum. In the Plantasia Hothouse you can marvel at the multitude of botanical specimens and associated creatures or for a spot of exercise and aquatic excitement visit the LC centre. At the Dylan Thomas Centre you can learn about the work and turbulent life of Swansea's most famous son.

Moving away from the Maritime Quarter into the city centre, the castle, hemmed in by the modern city and a shadow of its former self, is nevertheless a reminder of Swansea's long history. Close by Castle Square is the indoor market, the largest in Wales and an experience not to be missed; try some local cockles or laverbread, a type of seaweed and local delicacy. There are shops aplenty of course and for food and drink the Wind Street area has a plethora of cafes, restaurants and bars.

Swansea has lots of attractions that children will love. Many can be found alongside the promenade: Singleton Park has a boating lake with red dragon pedaloes; Blackpill Lido is a shallow waterpark, a great attraction on a fine summer's day; from Blackpill the Bay Rider land train sets off for Mumbles with its amusements, pier and ice cream parlours. Adults and children alike can walk, cycle or even roller blade on the traffic free and flat five mile route of the prom.

Top: Sail Bridge, Swansea; Bottom: The city centre at night

Swansea is proud of its parks and gardens and with just cause; there are over 50 green spaces in the city. Close to the city centre Cwmdonkin Park is known for its natural beauty and links to Dylan Thomas and there are two stunning botanical gardens, at Clyne Gardens and at Singleton Park.

Places to visit

National Waterfront Museum

Oystermouth Road
Maritime Quarter
SA1 3RD
☎ 01792 638950

The story of Swansea's and Wales' industrial past is told in this new museum, opened in 2005, part of the National Museum of Wales. Housed in a spectacular glass and slate building, linked to an original waterfront warehouse, the museum contains industrial artifacts large and small and combined with state of the art methods of presentation tells its story in a way which will keep adults and children enthralled; a must see attraction for all visitors to the city.

Dylan Thomas Centre

Somerset Place
SA1 1RR
☎ 01792 463980

The magnificent former Guildhall is home to the Dylan Thomas Centre, Learn about the life and work of Wales' most famous poet and playwright who was born and raised in the city.

LC centre

Oystermouth Road
SA1 3ST
☎ 01792 466500
www.thelcswansea.com

The LC centre is an up-to-the-minute leisure centre in three parts; the Edge offers water based fun for all the family with exciting state of the art rides to suit all ages, even including a surfing pool; the Core has an extensive children's play area, a multipurpose sports hall and a climbing wall; the Peak is a well equipped fitness centre.

Plantasia

Parc Tawe
SA1 2AL
☎ 01792 474555

A striking pyramidal glasshouse is home to thousands of exotic plants, fish, reptiles, butterflies and even monkeys; whatever the temperature outside, in Plantasia's hothouse it's always...well, hot.

Clyne Gardens

Mayals Road, Black Pill
SA3 5AR
☎ 01792 401737

Developed by the wealthy Vivian family in the late 19th and early 20th century this stunning botanical garden contains thousands of specimens, many sourced by the family from all over the world. Particularly notable are the architectural features, such as the Japanese Bridge, the bog garden, the oak woodland, and the extensive collection of rhododendrons and azaleas.

Glyn Vivian Art Gallery

Alexandra Road
SA1 5DZ
☎ 01792 516900

This prestigious gallery, based on the collections of Richard Glyn Vivian (1835-1910) and other beneficiaries, includes works by Richard Wilson, Claude Monet, Augustus John and contemporary Welsh artists. There is also an important collection of international porcelain and Swansea china as well as an ever changing programme of visiting exhibitions.

Swansea Museum

Victoria Road, Maritime Quarter
SA1 1SN
☎ 01792 653763

This museum, the oldest in Wales, is housed in an imposing neo-classical building and contains a diverse range of historical artifacts from Swansea and around the world.

Attractions Nearby

Mumbles Pier (6m/9.5km)

Mumbles Road, Mumbles
SA3 4EN
☎ 01792 365200
www.mumbles-pier.co.uk
Enjoy traditional seaside fun at the 738ft/225m long Victorian pier with a variety of amusements, spectacular views over Swansea Bay and its own private beach.

Margam Country Park (11.5m/18km)

Margam, Port Talbot
SA13 2TJ
☎ 01639 881635
You may need to set aside a whole day to do justice to this 1000 acre park. Attractions which will keep all the family amused include the ornamental gardens, the gothic styled mansion, the large deer herd, the adventure playground, the farm trail, the 18th century orangery and a range of walking trails.

Hotels and Dining

Try the local Tourist Information Centre, see Essential Contacts for details.

Something Special

Morgans Hotel

Somerset Place
SA1 1RR
☎ 0800 988 3001
www.morganshotel.co.uk
Imposing brick building, once home to the port authority, now operating as a stylish boutique hotel. In a superb location next to the Dylan Thomas Centre and the River Tawe.

The Dragon Hotel

The Kingsway
SA1 5LS
☎ 01792 657100
www.dragon-hotel.co.uk
A swimming pool and well equipped gym are attractions at this recently refurbished city centre hotel.

The Grand Hotel

Ivey Place, High Street
SA1 1NX
☎ 01792 645898
www.thegrandhotelswansea
The stylish modern interior belies the imposing 1930s facade. For that extra touch of luxury try a penthouse, with a roof top hot tub. This hotel couldn't be more convenient for rail travellers as it's situated adjacent to Swansea Rail Station.

Crescent Guest House

132 Eaton Crescent, Uplands
SA1 4QR
☎ 01792 465782
www.crescentguesthouse.co.uk
Comfortable guest house accommodation in large Edwardian house with superb views over the city.

Hanson at the Chelsea Restaurant

17 Mary Street
SA1 3LH
☎ 01792 464068
Intimate award winning restaurant at the heart of the city.

Mermaid Restaurant

686 Mumbles Road, Mumbles
SA3 4EE
☎ 01792 367744
Specialises in locally sourced produce such as salt marsh lamb from Gower.

Events

Dylan Thomas Festival

Swansea Festival of Music and the Arts

Mumbles Mostly Jazz and Blues Festival

Clyne in Bloom

Outdoor Shakespeare at Oystermouth Castle

Essential Contacts

Tourist Information Centre
Plymouth Street
SA1 3QG
☎ 01792 468321

The Grand Theatre
Singleton Street
SA1 3QJ
☎ 01792 475715
Grand by name and grand by nature this restored late Victorian theatre offers a full programme of drama, comedy and music.

Dylan Thomas Theatre
Gloucester Place
Maritime Quarter
SA1 1TY
☎ 01792 473238
Home to the Swansea Little Theatre amateur drama group and host to touring productions.

Tenby, Pembrokeshire

Getting There

By Road
Take the M4 and A40 to St Clears then theA477 and A478 to Tenby.

By Rail
Change at Swansea for trains to Tenby.

By Coach
National coaches serve Tenby.

Top and middle: Tenby Harbour;
Bottom: Tenby beach

Background Briefing

Tenby is a pretty, much photographed seaside resort in south Pembrokeshire. Dinbych-y-Pysgod, its Welsh name, means town of little fishes and although it has a picturesque harbour its fishing industry has now been superseded by the tourist industry. Set on a rocky headland and protected by its mediaeval wall on the landward side, the old town with its cobbled streets and colour washed Georgian houses and small shops is an attractive place. In the summer the streets are closed to traffic between 11am and 5pm which enables the many restaurants, pubs and cafes to spill out on to the streets creating a relaxed continental atmosphere.

The town was established by the Normans, on a former Welsh stronghold, as a fortified town with a castle. Little remains of the castle now but the mediaeval town wall with its unique five arches barbican gate still remains enclosing the old town. There are several ancient restored cannon on Castle Hill, which were used in times past to defend the town. St Mary's Church, a landmark in the town, is one of the oldest in Wales, the oldest part the tower being built about 700 years ago with the spire added some 200 years later.

Tenby's four beaches are second to none with miles of beautiful sand, all having won awards, including the prestigious Blue Flag award, for cleanliness and facilities. Boat trips and jetski safaris are available from Tenby Harbour, including fishing expeditions, seal and bird watching trips and boat crossings to the monastery on Caldy Island. Sail boats, pedalos and motor boats can also be hired from the harbour

The surrounding countryside and coastline are a magnet to walkers and cyclists alike, offering stunning views, rugged coastline with wildlife aplenty and quiet country roads.

There are a number of large tourist attractions nearby. The Dinosaur Park is on the way to St Florence, Heathertons Sports Park is a mile further along the same road and Manor House Wildlife Park is on the opposite side of the road. Folly Farm is about 5m/8km away to the north.

Places to visit

Tudor Merchants House (NT)
Quay Hill, Tenby
SA70 7BX
☎ 01834 842279
www.nationaltrust.org.uk
15th century three storey house within the town walls, illustrates how a Tudor family would have lived at the time. Features of the building include a 'Flemish' round chimney and original scarfed roof-trusses. There is also a small herb garden.

Tenby Museum & Art Gallery
Castle Hill , Tenby
SA70 7BP
☎ 01834 842 809
www.tenbymuseum.org.uk
Situated in a Grade II listed building, part of the old castle, there are five main galleries in the museum. They display the story of Tenby from the 10th to 21st centuries, Tenby's maritime history, geological and archaeological exhibits and two art galleries.

Caldy Island

Off Tenby
SA70 7UJ
☎ 01834 844453
www.caldey-island.co.uk
Caldy Island is home to an order of Cistercian monks, following a long tradition as the island has been inhabited by monks since Celtic times. The monks produce chocolate, shortbread and perfumes which are on sale to visitors. You can explore the historic Old Priory and the medieval churches or join the free guided walk for a closer look at the island's heritage. At the Video Centre you can find out more about life in the Monastery and visitors can attend one of the services in the Abbey Church. There is a beach, a tea garden and a walk up to the lighthouse giving splendid views.

From Easter to October boats are every 20 minutes from Tenby Harbour. Closed Sundays.

Attractions Nearby

Bosherston Lily Ponds (NT) (12m/19.5km)

National Trust Estate Office
Old Home Farm, Stackpole
SA71 5DQ
☎ 01646 661359
www.nationaltrust.org.uk/main/
w-stackpole-wildlife_walk.pdf
Take the six mile wildlife walk on the Stackpole estate including the lily ponds, created between 1780 and 1860 by flooding three narrow valleys. Download a leaflet from the NT website.

Colby Woodland Gardens (NT) (9m/14km)

Amroth
SA67 8PP
☎ 01834 811885
www.nationaltrust.org.uk
Set in a secluded valley the woodland garden is best seen in spring when the many rhododenrons and azaleas

are flowering. There is also a walled garden and gazebo and there are lots of walks with woodland, meadows and meandering streams to explore.

Hotels and Dining

Try the local Tourist Information Centre, see Essential Contacts for details.

Something Special

Elm Grove Country House (4m/6.5km)

St. Florence, Nr. Tenby
SA70 8LS
☎ 01834 871255
www.elmgrovecountryhouse.
co.uk
Elm Grove is a WTB 4 star Georgian Country House set among 20 acres of grounds just 4m/7km from Tenby. The unique character of this country house and its beautiful surroundings provide a memorable stay. Guests can expect traditional recipes and fresh local produce for breakfast and evening meals.

Heywood Mount Hotel

Heywood Lane, Tenby
SA70 8DA
☎ 01834 842087
www.heywoodmount.co.uk
Standing in one acre of grounds half a mile from the centre of town, Tenby's only WTB 4 star hotel offers quality accommodation, good food and friendly service. The restaurant has the coveted Fine Dining Award. Spa and leisure facilities include fitness gym, swimming pool, jacuzzi and sauna.

Atlantic Hotel

The Esplanade, Tenby
SA70 7DU
☎ 01834 842881
www.atlantic-hotel.uk.com
The Atlantic Hotel is a WTB and AA 3 star hotel; it has one of Tenby's finest views with cliff top gardens and panoramic views of the

South Beach, Caldey Island and the well known landmarks of Castle Hill and the island fort of St. Catherine. The hotel has a leisure spa with heated indoor pool, spa bath and steam room. The restaurant serves a modern European menu.

The Mews Bistro

Upper Frog Street, Tenby
SA70 7JD
☎ 01834 844068
www.mewsbistrotenby.co.uk
Specialising in locally caught fish the bistro also serves a full menu for the meat eater and vegetarian.

Events

Tenby Arts Festival

September

Tenby Blues Festival

November

Tregaron and the Ceredigion Coast

Getting There

By Road

Tregaron is on the A485 Aberystwyth to Lampeter road. The A487 Aberystwyth to Cardigan road serves places along the coast.

By Rail

The nearest railway station is at Aberystwyth then onward by local bus.

By Coach

There is a coach service to Aberystwyth.

Talbot Inn Tregaron

Background Briefing

The county of Ceredigion occupies a central position on Cardigan Bay. It is a mainly pastoral land of gently rolling countryside, small villages and towns, and quiet roads; but it also has a fine stretch of unspoiled coastline and to the east wild moorland.

The small country town of Tregaron nestles at the foot of this high land, a significant barrier to travel, crossed only by the narrow road across the wildly beautiful Abergwesyn Pass. The No1 mountain road in Wales (*The Times* survey). The town is a quiet place, apparently little troubled by the outside world and proud of its Welsh heritage. Its attractions are mainly to be found out of doors; Cors Caron nature reserve for its wild flowers and bird life; the Elenydd, a vast tract of open moorland and forest, uninhabited, wild and desolate at times, perfect for adventurous walking trips; the Ystwyth Trail, an excellent off road cycle route following the track of an old railway.

Tregaron does however have two indoor attractions that shouldn't be missed. The Red Kite Centre, housed in the old school, despite its name is not predominately about the local bird of prey. It is in fact a museum of local life; run by volunteers it gives a gentle introduction to the life and times of the area and makes a good first stop for visitors. The other must see attraction in town is the Rhiannon Welsh Gold Centre; with the chance to take home locally made high quality jewellery.

A short drive down quiet country roads from Tregaron leads to Aberaeron. This stylish small town of handsome, colourfully painted Georgian houses was built around the then commercial harbour just over two hundred years ago. It's a pleasant place with shops, cafes and a range of accommodation providers, making it a useful base for touring the area. It does however lack a good beach but some excellent sandy beaches can be found just a short distance to the south at New Quay, Cwmtydu, Llangranog and Penbryn. New Quay is also the place to go to see the delightful dolphins which frequent these waters, either on a boat trip or if you are lucky from the harbour wall.

Places to visit

Rhiannon

The Welsh Gold Centre
Main Square, Tregaron
SY25 6JL
☎ 01974 298415
Rhiannon Evans established her jewellery business in Tregaron in 1971. Since then the business has established an international reputation for excellence of design and quality of workmanship in its Celtic themed products, fashioned in gold and silver on the premises. Visitors can see the craftsmen at work and browse the extensive range of jewellery on display. There is also a craft centre selling fine craft work from around Wales and other Celtic countries, and a Welsh tea room.

The Red Kite Centre

Dewi Road, Tregaron
SY25 6JW

This is a charming local museum, an outpost of Ceredigion Museum. Staffed by friendly volunteers it's a good place to start a visit to Tregaron. Find out about local history, Tregaron Bog, including the latest bird sightings, and of course there's a display on the magnificent bird of prey from which it takes its name. The museum is housed in an old school and a major feature is a re-creation of a Victorian school classroom, complete with blackboard and easel.

Tregaron Bog (Cors Caron)

Enjoy a leisurely stroll down the old railway line, visit the observation tower, and observe the flora and fauna of this nature reserve.

The Elenydd

Experienced walkers can devise a route through the wild and desolate moorland of the Elenydd, to the east of Tregaron.

Attractions Nearby

Llanerchaeron (NT) (16m/25.5km)

Ciliau Aeron, Aberaeron
SA48 8DG
☎ 01545 570200

Self sufficiency was the principle on which this estate was established in the late 18th century. Attached to the John Nash designed mansion is a service courtyard which contains a dairy, salting house, laundry and even a brewery; fruit and vegetables were produced in two walled gardens. Over the last twenty years since it acquired the property the National Trust has painstakingly restored the estate to its former glory. There are attractive gardens with a lake, woodland walks, and a chance to observe work on the organic farm.

New Quay (24m/39km)

This small resort has steep streets with brightly painted old houses, a fine sandy beach, popular in the summer, and a harbour with moored yachts. Dolphins are commonly seen in the area and boat operators offer trips to observe these graceful animals. The poet Dylan Thomas lived in the town for a time and it provided inspiration for his writing. Walkers can enjoy the coast path; a steep zigzag path climbs up from the town leading to the crest of high cliffs with exposed beds of contorted sedimentary rock and continues along the cliffs to the secluded beach at Cwmtydu.

Strata Florida Abbey (7m/11km)

Explore the ruins of this once great abbey, set in marvellous countryside to the north of Tregaron.

Hotels and Dining

Try the local Tourist Information Centre, see Essential Contacts for details.

The Talbot Hotel

Tregaron
SY25 6JL
☎ 01974 298208
www.talbothotel-tregaron.com
This hotel on the town square is at the heart of the community. An old drover's inn with stone walls, oak beams and open fires.

Glanafon Guesthouse (4m/7km)

Llangeitho, Tregaron
SY25 6TL
☎ 01974 821546
www.glanafon-guesthouse.co.uk

Bryn Heulog B+B (4m/7km)

Llanddewi Brefi, Tregaron
SY25 6PE
☎ 01570 493615
www.brynheulog.com

Ty Mawr Mansion Country House (10.5m/17km)

Cilcennin, Lampeter
SA48 8BD
☎ 01570 470033
www.tymawrmansion.co.uk
This award winning luxury hotel in a grade II listed building overlooking the Aeron Valley offers spacious rooms with sumptuous furnishings, extensive grounds and it even has its own 27 seat cinema.

Feathers Royal Hotel (16.5m/27km)

Alban Square, Aberaeron
SA46 0AQ
☎ 01545 571750
feathersroyalhotel.com
Tastefully modernised coaching inn in the centre of town offering style with informality.

Harbourmaster (16.5m/27km)

Pen Cei, Aberaeron
SA46 0BT
☎ 01545 570755
www.harbour-master.com
Chic hotel with rooms overlooking the harbour. Seafood is a speciality in the restaurant along with Welsh Black beef and locally sourced lamb.

Castle Hotel (16.5m/27km)

20 Market Street, Aberaeron
SA46 0AU
☎ 01545 570205
www.the-castlehotel.co.uk
Comfortable hotel close by the picturesque harbour.

The Hungry Trout (24m/39km)

2 South John Street, New Quay
SA45 9NG
☎ 01545 560680
www.thehungrytrout.co.uk
Notable seafood restaurant close by New Quay's sea front.

Events

Aberaeron Festival of Ponies and Cobs

Tregaron Festival of Harness Racing

Essential Contacts

Aberaeron Tourist Information Centre
The Quay, Aberaeron
SA46 0BT
☎ 01545 570602

Cardigan Bay Marine Wildlife Centre
Glanmor Terrace, New Quay
SA45 9PS
☎ 01545 560032
Dolphin spotting boat trips

New Quay Boat Trips
The Moorings, Glanmor Terrace
SA45 9PS
☎ 01545 560800
Dolphin spotting and fishing trips

Top: Powys Castle; Bottom: Welshpool and Llanfair Light Railway

Background Briefing

Lying on the western slopes of the Severn valley, four miles from the English border, the historic market town of Welshpool provides a good base from which to explore the many attractions of northern Powys. The town was known originally simply as Pool, possibly after a feature on the River Severn, the prefix being added later to avoid confusion with Poole in Dorset.

Its principal occupation over the ages has been to serve the agricultural community around it. The market tradition goes back centuries and continues today with the indoor market held in the Town Hall on Saturdays and Mondays, with a farmers market on the first Friday of each month. The Smithfield Livestock Market, held on Mondays, is the largest one day livestock market in Wales, and one of the largest in Europe for sheep.

There are several historic buildings to be found in the town, many of which can be seen by following the Heritage Trail (pick up a leaflet at the TIC); these include timber framed buildings dating back to the 16th century. Something of an oddity is the Cockpit; specially erected in the 18th century for cock fighting, it was used until 1849 when the activity was made illegal.

The town's prosperity was greatly increased by transport improvements, firstly by the arrival of the canal in 1796, then by the railway in 1862. A recent slight realignment of the railway line to ease the building of a new bypass means that the rather grand old station building now has an alternative function as a popular restaurant and retail outlet; but trains do still stop at a new station a short distance away. The Montgomery Canal passes close to the centre of town; closed in 1944, much of the canal has since been restored by enthusiasts and now provides a fine amenity, in effect a linear nature reserve where the towpath provides the opportunity to stroll in a tranquil environment, surrounded by a

Town Hall Welshpool

diverse range of birds, insects, plants and aquatic life.

Just outside town, Powis Castle is one of mid Wales' most popular tourist attractions, not only for the grandeur of the building and its sumptuous furnishings but also for the splendid gardens. Running from Raven Square on the western edge of town the Welshpool and Llanfair Light Railway will delight visitors of all ages with its sixteen mile round trip in open carriages behind a steam locomotive.

Places to visit

Powysland Museum

The Canal Wharf, Welshpool
SY21 7AQ
☎ 01938 554656

A museum of rural life depicting life in Welshpool and Montgomeryshire through the ages by means of artifacts, maps and old photographs in the setting of a former canal warehouse.

Powis Castle and Garden (NT)

Welshpool
SY21 8RF
☎ 01938 551944

This magnificent red stone edifice, on its rocky ridge, dominates the countryside around. Founded in medieval times by the princes of Powys the castle has been remodelled and embellished over 700 years to meet the requirements of succeeding generations, remaining in continuous occupation, first as a stronghold, then as a stately home. It contains a rich collection of furniture, paintings and sculpture acquired by the Herbert and Clive families, including a collection of treasures from India once belonging to Robert Clive, whose son married into the Herbert family.

The opulence of the stately castle is matched by the splendour of the world famous gardens. The terraced Baroque gardens are adorned with original lead statues and contain an orangery and aviary. Ancient clipped yew hedges shelter unusual and tender plants. The original kitchen garden has been converted into a flower garden, a riot of colour in the summer months. Be sure to allow yourself plenty of time to savour the multitude of delights on offer at Powis Castle and gardens.

Welshpool & Llanfair Light Railway

The Station, Llanfair Caereinion
Welshpool
SY21 0SF
☎ 01938 810441
www.wllr.org.uk

This charming narrow gauge railway runs from Welshpool to the sleepy village of Llanfair Caereinion. As the diminutive steam locomotive battles with steep gradients and tight bends passengers can sit back and watch the lush countryside of the Banwy valley slip by.

Attractions Nearby

Glansevern Hall Gardens (5.5m/8.5km)

Berriew
SY21 8AH
☎ 01686 640644

Garden lovers will delight in the sights and scents of this mature 20 acre garden with its unusual trees, sculptures, grotto and lakeside walks.

Silver Scenes (5.5m/8.5km)

Berriew SY21 8QA
☎ 01686 640695

Established in the mid 80s Silver Scenes design and manufacture quality pewter and silver plated giftware. Browse the full range of their products in the shop or take a guided tour of the factory to see the production process.

Breidden Hills (8m/12.5km)

The three peaks of the Breidden hills straddle the Welsh border just to the north of Welshpool. The highest point is topped by Rodney's Pillar, a monument to commemorate Admiral Rodney who defeated the French fleet in the West Indies in the 18th century. His ships were built using local wood, shipped down the River Severn to Bristol. A footpath climbs steeply from the car park at Criggion to the monument, from where there are panoramic views over mid Wales and Shropshire.

Lake Vyrnwy (22.5m/36km)

Lake Vyrnwy lies in a secluded location on the eastern slopes of the Berwyn mountain range; built in the late 19th century as a reservoir to supply water to Liverpool the massive stone dam holds back an area of water the size of 600 football pitches. Now it is a popular tourist destination with something for everyone. Wander round the sculpture park with its fascinating wooden constructions, visit a bird hide or follow a trail to observe the wealth of bird life in the RSPB reserve, hire a bike for a leisurely pedal round the 12m/19km long circumference of the lake, browse the craft shops or relax with a coffee in one of the teashops. Other activities available include canoeing, clay pigeon shooting and fishing.

Hotels and Dining

Try the local Tourist Information Centre, see Essential Contacts for details.

Royal Oak Hotel

The Cross, Welshpool
SY21 7DG
☎ 01938 552217
www.royaloakhotel.info

Welshpool, Powys (Continued)

Once part of the Powis Castle estate this grade II listed building offers up to date hotel facilities in the centre of town.

Hafren House B+B
38 Salop Road
SY21 7EA
☎ 01938 555148
www.hafrenhouse.com
Comfortable guest house near the town centre.

Edderton Hall Country House (3.5m/5.5km)
Forden, Welshpool
SY21 8RZ
☎ 01938 580339
www.eddertonhall.com
A luxury guest house in a Georgian mansion surrounded by beautiful countryside in the Severn valley.

The Lion Hotel (5.5m/8.5km)
Berriew
SY21 8PQ
☎ 01686 640452
Oak beams and wattle and daub add to the atmosphere at this 17th century village inn with food served in the cosy dining room.

Landmark Trust
Poultry Cottage
Former estate cottage, sleeps up to 4.

Events

Welshpool Festival of Transport

Country Music Festival

Welsh Food Festival

Gwyl Gregynog Festival (classical music)

Essential Contacts

Tourist Information Centre
The Vicarage Gardens Car Park
Church Street
☎ 01938 552043

Artisans
The Old Sawmill, Lake Vyrnwy
Llanwddyn
SY10 0NA
☎ 01691 870317
www.artisans-lakevyrnwy.co.uk
Cycle hire

Bethania Adventure
Capel Bethania, Llanwddyn, Oswestry
SY10 0NJ
☎ 01691 870615
Canoeing and other activities on and near Lake Vyrnwy.

Welsh Language

Wales has a rich cultural heritage and its own language, Welsh, one of the oldest European languages. It is the first language of about one quarter of the population in Wales, as a general rule the further west you go the more likely you are to hear Welsh spoken. Most signs are bi-lingual and you will come across the language all over Wales. Below is a list of the most common words you will find on maps and road signs.

Croeso i Gymru - Welcome to Wales
aber - river mouth
afon - river
bach - small
betws - chapel or oratory
blaen - head, end or source
bryn - hill
bwlch - mountain pass
cadair - stronghold
caer - fort or castle
canolfan hamdden - leisure centre
capel - chapel
castell - castle
cefn - ridge
coch - red

coed - wood or forest
cwm - valley
dinas - fort
du - black
dyffryn - valley
fford - road
glas - blue or green
glyn - glen
gwyn - white
llan - church, enclosure
llwyd - grey
llyn - lake
maes - field
melyn - yellow
moel - bare hill
môr - sea

morfa - coastal marsh
mynydd - mountain
nant - valley
ogof - cave
pentre - village
pont - bridge
pwll nofio - swimming pool
pistyll - waterfall
traeth - beach
tref - town
ynys - island
ysbyty - hospital
ysgol - school
ystrad - valley floor

Index

Index

Photograph acknowledgements

Courtesy of Amgueddfa Cymru National Museum Wales: Cover (back, top), 9 bottom, 13 top-left
Rita & David Pearson: Cover (back, third down), 8 middle, 25 bottom-left, 28 bottom, 31
The National Wool Museum: 8 bottom-right; 77 top-right
Helen Maurice-Jones: 8 bottom-left
Nick Turner/CAT: 9 top
Stephen Hopkins: 48 bottom
National Botanic Garden of Wales: 56 top (both)
Aberglasney Hall and Gardens: 56 bottom-right
Clearwell Caves: 71 top-right

The images below are courtesy of www.shutterstock.com with copyright to:

Gail Johnson: Cover (front), 6 top, 6 bottom, 7 top, 22, 29, 32 bottom, 33t, 40 top-right, 40 middle;
Joe Goodson: 9 top-right; *Stephen Meese:* 19; *David Hughes:* 27 top & bottom, 28 top-left, 28 top-right, 53 top;
Carlos Neto: 32; *Darryl Sleath:* 34, 35; *Thierry Maffeis:* Cover (back, bottom-right), 9 top-left, 45 top, 46, 86 bottom;
Tom Curtis: 60 right, 61 right; *Groomsee:* 73 top; *Jon le-bon:* 83 top, 83 bottom, 84 top, 84 bottom;
Dave Massey: Cover (back, bottom-left), 86 top; *Adrian Phillips:* 86 middle

Lindsey Porter: All other photography